GEOCACHING
IN THE UK

ABOUT THE AUTHOR

Lancashire-based Terry Marsh is a full-time writer and photographer specialising in travel and the outdoors. He first became interested in geocaching while working on the Isle of Skye, and responded to his son's challenge to write a book about it. Since then, while not admitting to being obsessed with the pursuit, he regularly tries to fit geocaching forays into research trips for books he's working on.

Terry is the author of several books for Cicerone Press (from a total of more than 70 written over the years), and uses geocaching as an excuse not to retire.

Other Cicerone guides by the author

Great Mountain Days in Snowdonia
The Isle of Mull
The Isle of Skye
The West Highland Way
A Northern Coast-to-Coast Walk
The Dales Way

The Shropshire Way (with Julie Meech)
Walking on the Isle of Man
Walking in the Forest of Bowland and
  Pendle
Walking on the West Pennine Moors

GEOCACHING IN THE UK

by
Terry Marsh

2 POLICE SQUARE, MILNTHORPE, CUMBRIA, LA7 7PY
www.cicerone.co.uk

© Terry Marsh 2011
First edition 2011
ISBN: 978 1 85284 609 1

Printed by KHL Printing, Singapore
A catalogue record for this book is availal
All photographs are by the author unless

*This book is dedicated to my son, Martin
book about geocaching?' in front of me, v*

ACKNOWLEDGEMENTS

Geocaching is a developing pursuit, and to give a meaningful overview I have called on a number of people who have kindly given me assistance in the writing of this book.

John Stead, one of the first geocachers in the UK, very generously offered to read the entire manuscript, although I doubt he knew what he was letting himself in for. Nevertheless, he did so unfailingly and offered sensible advice as well as picking up on my errors. I am very grateful for his contribution. Dave Palmer (deceangi), one of the most experienced and respected reviewers, made me an offer I couldn't refuse – to read through the manuscript. He gave me very helpful advice and some historical information, which was both appreciated and taken on board.

Groundspeak, the founding organisation, have given permission to use screen shots from the www.geocaching.com website, along with consent to use trademark logos. They have also generously supplied pictures of geocaching merchandise pages. The Geological Society of America has kindly given consent to use the EarthCache name and logos. Garmin UK have generously given permission to use illustrations of their GPS devices (page 19); Groundspeak, Trimble, Memory Map and SatMap have given permission to use images on page 21.

Others, especially colleagues in North West Caching, have helped in small but no less important ways. Jeanette Hindle agreed to my use of her geocoin design shown on page 18; Ian Grime gave consent to use his 10-10-10 design on pages 53 and 119; members of the north-west community supplied many of the other colourful pictures of geocoins scattered across the margins of the book; and my son, Martin, took the photograph of my grandson on page 90, and of me on page 45.

Especial thanks goes to my wife, Viv, who says geocaching is the best thing we've ever done, because now we go out walking together much more often, and visit places neither of us have ever seen before.

DISCLAIMER

Front cover: A family search for a geocache.

CONTENTS

Malham Cove in the Yorkshire Dales National Park is a perfect example of an EarthCache

INTRODUCTION

Everyone dreams of finding treasure – a crock of gold at the end of a rainbow, a rare antique of singular value or an undiscovered Wordsworth manuscript. Such is, indeed, the stuff of dreams. Yet the laws of probability dictate that it's extremely unlikely to happen.

For those with less exalted ambition, treasure is all around, just waiting to be found. What is more, very accurate and detailed clues have been left as to where to find it. It may not bring life-changing riches, for the value of this treasure lies in its discovery – not in its quantifiable worth.

Geocaching is essentially a modern form of treasure hunting. Of course, the game of treasure hunting has been around for centuries. In its simplest form, it involves being given a list of objects to find and bring back – the first one back with everything wins. A more sophisticated version involves unravelling clues to the whereabouts of hidden 'treasure', and then heading off to find it. The same holds true of the next stage in the development of the pursuit – letterboxing – which started on Dartmoor in the mid-1800s and followed much the same principle.

With today's technology, treasure hunting has developed yet again into the activity of geocaching – a cross between treasure hunting and orienteering. Started in the US in the year 2000, when the first 'geocache' was hidden and its location posted on the internet for others to find with a GPS, geocaching has now become a worldwide phenomenon.

Anyone can join in – all you need is access to the website where geocache locations are listed (or, in a more sophisticated version, a series of clues to a location).

Caches can be found almost on your own doorstep, and certainly within a short distance of where you live.

Simply choose a geocache, take your GPS and go out and find the spot. Once you get to its location, the fun really starts, as the geocache is often cleverly hidden. And it is important that no one else (that is, a non-geocacher, or 'muggle', a term borrowed from the Harry Potter books) sees you find it. It may be in a town or other busy place, but caches are more often hidden in the countryside. (All the full-page pictures in this book are of places where someone has placed a geocache or locations which are EarthCaches.)

When you find the geocache – it's likely to be in a small plastic box – have a look at what's inside. It could be just a logbook to record your find, or there may be other items too. You can take these as your treasure, as long as you replace any items you take with others of equal or greater value. Then hide the cache (without any muggles seeing) where you found it, so that others can enjoy searching for it, and go home to record your find on the website.

That's it, fundamentally at least; there is no other achievement. But unlike train spotting, for example, which is largely a chance activity, successful geocaching hinges on your own ability to find the location of the cache. With geocaching, you are the search engine.

But, be warned; it is addictive. Once you find your first few caches, so the urge to find more grows, and every trip out (even in your local town) or visit to the countryside suddenly offers the possibility of finding another cache.

WHAT'S IN A CACHE?

Many traditional caches include trinkets, of no real value, which can be swapped – 'take something out, put something in' is a founding rule. Other caches provide a series of clues that lead round notable sites – they may be of historical significance or perhaps illustrate aspects of rural life.

Caches may contain some items that have been invented specifically for the activity as it has grown. Known as 'travel bugs' and 'geocoins', these items have a 'mission' assigned by the owner – usually to travel around the world via caches, or more specifically, for example, to visit mountains or other caches in an alphabetical sequence.

Once a travel bug or geocoin is retrieved from a cache, its discovery is logged on the geocaching website, where its own page and its stated mission can be discovered. It is then for the finder to comply with the mission statement, and move the item on accordingly. What makes this simple endeavour all the more appealing is that, via the website, the progress of each item can be tracked and displayed on a map, enabling children in particular to experience a lesson in regional, national and world geography.

OTHER BENEFITS OF GEOCACHING

In addition to being a fun activity, there is a growing realisation that geocaching has a number of bolt-on benefits. Firstly, it need not be a solitary pursuit – many geocachers go out with friends or in family groups, involving children, parents and grandparents in the enjoyment of our countryside in a pleasurable and healthy way. It is also a great way to spend retirement days.

In parts of the country local geocachers organise social events, maybe a visit to a pub, or a walk to coincide with solstices or significant historical events. Such 'cache events' are commonplace, and provide yet another opportunity to socialise and interact with like-minded individuals.

In fact, geocaching gets us all out walking and adds a new dimension to a walk. Often, the search for geocaches, even close to your home, will take you to places you probably never knew existed, a small local park, maybe, or a corner of woodland rarely visited.

Geocaching is for all the family – young and old alike

Geocaching keeps you in touch with nature – and with your friends! (photo: Mark Fishwick)

Educationalists in America, and organisations such as the National Trust and various local authorities in the UK, are using geocaching as a way of putting a new slant on learning by giving children GPS devices and getting them to navigate to a given location, where the teacher then explains the significance of the spot – in historical, geological or local terms – before moving on to the next location. Not only do the children get the lesson they were going to be given anyway, but they learn how to handle new technology and to navigate using satellite systems. Learning suddenly acquires an additional level of interest.

Geocaching can also be useful as a team-building exercise for those in company management.

Today, it is mind-boggling to think that there are tens of thousands of geocaches within the UK, and over one million worldwide. So popular is the pursuit becoming that the number of new caches worldwide is increasing by more than a thousand every week, and there are almost two million 'finds' every month. Judging by the comments left in logbooks and on the website, huge fun and enjoyment is derived from it.

And – whether you're searching near your home or on a visit to the countryside – you'll never look at your environment in the same way again. Every walk in the park with the dog, every trip to the countryside, and perhaps every visit to the supermarket leads past a concealed geocache that most folk would simply never know was there. So get out and see what treasure you can find!

The Cantilever, a fine EarthCache on the summit of Glyder Fach in Snowdonia National Park

1 THE BASICS

WHAT IS GEOCACHING?

Put simply, geocaching is a cross between treasure hunting and orienteering, but at a leisurely pace. It is, after all, a leisure pursuit – an adjunct to recreational walking that adds a new dimension to a visit to the countryside or even to the supermarket.

Typically, a 'cache' takes the form of a plastic Tupperware-like box – one that can be locked against the weather. But there are a number of different types of cache, not all of them as obvious as a large plastic box. A cache is concealed, often ingeniously, in some not-easy-to-stumble-upon location – away from a regular path, for example – and its exact location is uploaded to the internet (www.geocaching.com or, more UK-specific but less well known, www.opencaching.org.uk – see Chapter 10) so that others may then discover it using a hand-held GPS device and a little ingenuity. Traditional caches such as these usually contain a logbook and pencil to enable finders to record their discovery, which they later also put on the website.

THE HISTORY OF GEOCACHING

The modern leisure pursuit of geocaching (pronounced gee-o-cash-ing) became a possibility only when what is known as 'selective availability' – a policy adopted by the US Department of Defense to introduce some intentional 'noise' into their Global Positioning System (GPS) satellite signals in order to degrade their accuracy for civilian users – was removed from civilian GPS devices in 2000 (see Chapter 2). Until then GPS units, other than those used for military purposes, were neither precise nor useful. Suddenly, with a GPS device it became possible to pinpoint, very accurately, any given location using co-ordinates of both latitude and longitude. Once that became achievable, it was just one short step for outdoor mankind into the world of high-tech treasure hunting.

Geocaching owes a lot to both the traditional forms of treasure hunting and letterboxing (a treasure hunt that required you to decipher clues left in landmarks and printed materials). Today, geocaching uses technology and often (but not always) a series of clues to locate a position, or 'cache', or other piece of information.

Jack (The Magna Defender) finds Fozzie Bear (GC103JQ)

There are 'rules' covering the contents of caches, and items are required to be safe and suitable for all ages. If a cache is reported to contain questionable items, it can be temporarily disabled by a reviewer until the offending items are removed.

On 3 May 2000, an Oregon resident planted the first geocache. He posted the GPS location on a Usenet group, and it was found twice within three days. Geocaching was born, and the rest, as they say, is history.

In the UK, Hampshire County Council was the first local authority, and major landowner, in the UK to officially recognise geocaching as a great way of getting families and others out into the countryside, and as a valuable educational resource. In July 2003, Hampshire County Council, with members of the geocaching community, held what was the first organised geocaching event in the UK officially recognised by any major landowner, and open to members of the non-geocaching community. It took place at Farley Mount Country Park.

IS IT FOR YOU?

Geocaching is great for anyone who loves sight-seeing and leisure activities in the outdoors, and for those who, perhaps for health reasons, are looking for an enjoyable way to get some fresh air and exercise. It gives you an excuse to go off the beaten path and take notice of things around you, things that maybe you otherwise would take for granted. And geocaching is a pursuit that can be followed by all ages, from the youngest to those enjoying their retirement years.

Geocaching will also appeal to anyone who likes puzzles and challenges, because not all the cache information is readily given. You may find that you need to visit more than one location to acquire information that feeds into final co-ordinates, and/or that the information comes in the guise of cryptic, sometimes very cryptic, clues.

It also helps if you have a streak of the explorer or pirate in you – searching for treasure is what it's all about. Some people look on geocaching as playing with high-tech toys. In fact, geocaching is rather more of an adventure. You may have sophisticated tools at your disposal, but finding a geocache takes wits, know-how and patience. Geocaching is not like a board game where you can rely on strategies and chance. Instead, with geocaching, you need to be able to decipher clues left by those who hide the cache, and you must travel to the hidden cache as well. This requires time and can demand a reasonable level of physical fitness.

USING THE GEOCACHING WEBSITE

The principal key to geocaching is a website – www.geocaching.com – owned and managed by a business called Groundspeak, which is based in the US. So to take part in geocaching you need to have access to a computer with a web browser, and be moderately competent at using both.

The first thing to do is to register on the website and then 'invent' a name for yourself. There is nothing to stop you using your personal name, unless someone else has used the same name. But there is fun in devising a pseudonym under which you play the game. Take a look at some of the logs entered on the website to get the idea.

Five-baa-ed gate – when geocaching in rural areas, always observe the Countryside Code (see Appendix C) (photo: Mark Fishwick)

On the website, you can find information that tells you where there are geocaches in your locality, or indeed worldwide. You'll be surprised to find that you probably pass some on a daily basis.

Once you have found the information about geocaches, obtain co-ordinates from the website for each individual cache, which will tell you fairly precisely where the cache is hidden. Then all you have to do is go out and find it. When you get to the location, the cache won't be instantly obvious; most are well hidden and need to be searched for. But the search is all part of the fun, and all the more so because it is something that (according to geocaching 'rules') must be done away from prying eyes – in other words, do not search for, retrieve or replace a cache if anyone not in your group can see you. In this way, you prevent the cache from being removed or damaged, leaving it in place for the next geocacher to find. And, as some of the caches are intentionally in popular and busy locations, this in itself is often quite difficult, and at times impossible.

Having found a cache, enter your name in its logbook, along with the date, and then replace the cache. When you get home, record your find and write a few notes on the geocaching website. The website is remarkably ingenious and tots up your personal finds, keeping a life-long record of your geocaching activity.

Of course, there are times when you may not find your chosen geocache. Perhaps your search wasn't diligent enough, or the cache was found by a non-geocacher (or 'muggle'), or perhaps it was found by a fox that knocked it about a bit thinking there may be food in it. Then you need to record on the website the fact that you did not find it (DNF) to enable the 'owner' to investigate.

WHAT YOU NEED TO GET STARTED

The website gives co-ordinate information for caches in two forms: latitude and longitude; or a reference point from the British grid system. Of course, if you visit countries outside the UK the grid system is not applicable. In order to use the co-ordinate information you need a GPS device, a small hand-held instrument that uses satellite technology to locate your position, rather like a SatNav in a car. You can store cache co-ordinates on GPS devices, and then use the device to locate them. Using a GPS is not difficult, but neither is it intuitive – although a little practice goes a long way. When you arrive at your location, all you have to do is find the cache.

If you are adept at using a map and compass, then you don't even need a GPS, not in the UK at least, as the grid references are accurate enough to pinpoint the locality of the cache on a map. But, it has to be said, a GPS device can get you closer to your target than using grid references for the simple reason that the satellite system relays your position fairly accurately (using up to 12 satellite points of reference) and tells you when you arrive at the cache location, whereas using map and compass to achieve the same thing uses only two points of reference (northings and eastings), which requires a much higher degree of navigational skill.

So, all you need is a GPS device (see Chapter 2) and a basic understanding of the use of the internet, and off you go. Of course, that does not mean you should discard map and compass – they will still come in handy, if only to find your way around fields or across rivers.

As geocaching is an outdoor pursuit, it follows that you'll need adequate outdoor clothing, too, and a decent pair of walking boots, if you plan to seek out the more remote caches. There are caches on the summits of mountains, in caves, under bridges, beside rivers, deep in woodland cover and along canals – in fact, you may encounter all kinds of terrain, and need to be suitably equipped.

THE BASIC RULES OF GEOCACHING

As with any 'game', there are a few rules, but in the case of geocaching, they are few and uncomplicated.

- Having successfully arrived at the approximate location of the cache, do not look for it, retrieve it or replace it if you can be observed by non-geocachers (muggles).
- Sign the logbook with the date and your geocaching pseudonym. If the logbook is large enough, you may want to add a comment. If you are the first person to find the cache, you should also enter the time.
- If you wish to, feel free to take items from the cache (always exchange them for something of equal or greater value, unless they are items designed specifically to be taken and moved on) – some caches are too small to accommodate anything other than the log.
- Replace the cache exactly where you found it and conceal it appropriately. If you move the cache to a slightly different location, even if the co-ordinates are the same, you may have lessened the challenge for others and taken some of the fun out of it. Conversely, do not replace the cache in such a way that it becomes virtually impossible to find or retrieve.

Not all geocaches are easily accessible; for some you need to put in the effort to reach locations like Seathwaite Tarn in Cumbria

2

GPS DEVICES

Before you can take part in your first search for a geocache you need some basic tools. Although you can, theoretically, manage without it for some geocaches, you really need a GPS device, along with the co-ordinates of the cache you are looking for. It is also helpful to have a map of the area, and perhaps a compass, too, although most GPS devices have an in-built compass.

For aeons, man has looked to the sky to calculate his whereabouts. Traditionally, the sun and the fixed stars have been our guides. But today, constellations of man-made satellites have taken over as signals to guide our way.

THE GLOBAL POSITIONING SYSTEM (GPS) EXPLAINED

GPS satellites, powered by solar energy, orbit the Earth about twice a day, travelling about 11,000 miles above the planet and at some 7000mph (see diagram below). They were designed as a navigational system for military operations, but are now increasingly used for other activities. Each satellite sends out a unique radio signal, and a GPS

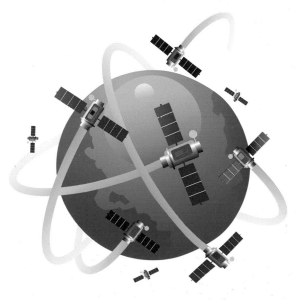

device on Earth can take readings and measurements from up to 24 satellites. It uses these to compute the distance to the satellite and so work out the location of the GPS. It is rare to get pinpoint accuracy, but for the purposes of geocaching this is not wholly necessary, as part of the fun is the 'hunt' once you get close.

The satellites are in such orbits that at any one time your GPS device can pick up signals from at least six, and often more, varying with time as satellites come in and out of 'view'. A display on the GPS shows how many satellites are being connected with. You need contact with at least four satellites to get a clear 3-D fix on location and altitude. Fewer than this and you get only a 2-D fix, but this, in general, is not a critical issue for geocaching unless you are seeking caches concealed on mountain summits.

At present, the US (GPS) and Russia (Glonass) provide the only global satellite navigation systems available. A third system, Galileo, is being built and operated in Europe, and should be fully functioning by 2014. The three systems will be completely integrated, which means that you will be able to determine a position by picking up signals from any combination of satellites belonging to any of the three systems.

Anyone can use the satellite system – it is completely free. The system has long been used by aircraft and shipping, but increasingly it is being used by surveyors, mapmakers, conservationists, mobile phone networks, emergency services, walkers and motorists.

SELECTING A GPS DEVICE

Although it is possible to spend a significant fortune on the most sophisticated GPS device, accurate in certain conditions to 1cm, such expense or accuracy is not necessary for geocaching. If your GPS receiver takes you to within 1cm of a cache, then some of the fun goes. It is searching for the concealed cache that is part of the game. So, something a bit more modest is perfectly acceptable.

But one thing is of key importance – no one device is significantly more accurate than another. So you can buy the cheapest and still enjoy the experiences of geocaching. Some of the more sophisticated ones, however, have additional features and are geocaching specific – that is, they are designed for geocaching and have added features to enable you to store cache co-ordinates and to record finds.

It is important to realise that a GPS device will direct you to the cache co-ordinates by the most direct route – a straight line – and this may be far from achievable, since the GPS takes no account of intervening rivers, valleys, mountains, forests, farm fields and sundry other obstructions. The

GPS will point you in the right direction, but you need to figure out for yourself how to get there. This is where a map and compass, and the ability to use both, comes in useful. Quite often you don't need a map and compass, but equally often you do, not least because they can ensure that you avoid trespassing.

In the UK, the principal suppliers of GPS devices is Garmin, and they have a wide range of instruments.

Garmin GPS devices

All GPS devices offer the same functionality, so any variation in price is entirely dependent on additional built-in features. Understanding your needs will help determine how you spend your money, although there is much to be said for acquiring a basic device first and then upgrading at some later stage once you have an idea of how the additional features (and expenditure) might best serve you. Considerations you might want to take into account are

- do I need my GPS to display maps?
- how much more helpful would it be to have a device that is geocaching compatible?
- in what type of terrain am I most likely to be using the GPS?
- is size and weight of any concern?
- what can I afford?

A word about geocaching compatibility

Basic GPS devices are not geocaching compatible; more sophisticated devices are. The latter will store your co-ordinate information in a special 'Geocaching' folder from which you can select your caches on the trail. It lists these caches in the order of those nearest to you, in a straight line. Once you have located the cache, you can tell the device that you have done so, and it will direct you to the next nearest cache without your having to scroll through the database. It can even be programmed to add your daily finds to the in-built calendar for later referencing, although these

entries will be simultaneously removed once you delete the cache record from the device. The most sophisticated GPS devices will also allow you to log your find directly to the website.

There is another issue. Most cache codes (the arrangement of numbers and letters beginning with 'GC' that identify the cache) have seven characters. Basic devices store only the first six of these characters, whereas more expensive devices store them all. The significance of this becomes apparent if you are following a series of caches placed by the same owner, all of which begin with the same first six characters, with only the final character being different. A basic device will store only one of the caches, and, if you try to send other similar codes to the device, it will simply overwrite the earlier entries. So, instead of having a series of caches in your GPS, you have only one. Devices that are geocaching compatible do not have this problem, and will download all the codes in full.

IPHONES AND BLACKBERRIES

Before you rush out and buy a GPS device, you might want to pause, especially if you own either an iPhone or a Blackberry. Both these devices are capable of downloading and operating geocaching software that works every bit as efficiently as a conventional GPS device. These applications use mobile broadband (3G or GPRS) to download information and are amazingly accurate. The software is not free, but is considerably cheaper than buying a new GPS device. But first, you do need to check that your iPhone or Blackberry has GPS capability and that this is activated on your account.

Where these applications score over conventional GPS devices is in offering additional functions, such as
- search by current location, address or cache code
- filter your own hides and finds from the www.geocaching.com search results
- access geocache details, including description, photo gallery, attributes, recent logs, hint and inventory
- look up trackable item details, including item goals, while on the trail (see Chapter 8)
- save geocache listings, including maps and photos, for quick retrieval and offline use
- log geocache finds and post notes or logs in the field
- download active Pocket Queries (see Chapter 9) for use while outside of network coverage
- view geocache web pages on www.geocaching.com without leaving the application, using embedded web browser.

There are advanced capabilities, too, which allow the user to

- view nearby caches on the embedded map
- view cache size, terrain and difficulty rating directly from the map screen
- navigate to geocaches with a simulated compass arrow (iPhone 3G and 3GS only) or directly from the map screen
- add custom waypoints when navigating to multi-caches
- switch between street, topographic and satellite maps.

Many of these features are included as standard in top-end conventional GPS devices. Of course, these particular applications are changing all the time, but the beauty of a mobile phone application is in the ability it provides – should you be away from your normal base, perhaps unexpectedly – to search for nearby caches to fill a spare moment.

Geocaching options also feature on other GPS devices, such as the SatMap Active 10 and Memory Map devices, which are primarily map-based tracking systems, but with geocaching options built in.

 No matter how expensive and sophisticated the GPS device you choose, if the cache owner used a basic device to calculate the co-ordinates, no amount of high-tech gadgetry is going to make your readings any more accurate. Think before you spend.

Displays of the iPhone geocaching application

Display of Memory Map Adventurer 2800

The SatMap
Active 10 GPS device

Displays from Navigator Trimble on Blackberry

The glaciated mountains of Cadair Idris in the Snowdonia National Park provide another great location for an EarthCache

ACCURACY AND LIMITATIONS OF GPS DEVICES

For all practical purposes, GPS devices are not affected by weather conditions or cloud cover. But to get an accurate and clear reading, GPS devices (and this includes the mobile phone applications) require a clear view of the sky in order to pick up satellite signals. Reception, and therefore accuracy, can be affected by woodland cover, the nearby presence of cliffs or tall buildings.

There are five main factors affecting GPS accuracy.

- **Ephemeris errors** occur when the satellite does not correctly transmit its exact position in orbit.
- **Ionosphere and troposphere conditions** can affect transmissions from the satellites.
- **Timing errors** are possible because, while the satellites each have an atomic clock (accurate to within 3 nanoseconds or 3-billionths of a second), the clock in your GPS device is significantly less accurate, and this can cause slight positional inconsistencies.
- **Multi-path errors** occur when a satellite signal bounces off a hard surface, such as a building or a cliff, before it reaches the receiver, causing a time delay and an inaccurate calculation of distance.
- **Poor satellite coverage** can occur when you do not have a wide and open view of the sky (which makes geocaching in cities much more difficult than in more open spaces).

Because a GPS device is an electronic instrument it relies on battery power. These can (and do) run down, so it is essential to carry spares at all times. Moreover, the instrument can be damaged or simply malfunction. Most of the dedicated GPS receivers are waterproof, but the same may not be true of mobile phone receivers.

GPS MEMORY

GPS devices have differing amounts of internal memory, and this will determine the number of waypoints, logs, routes and geocaching data you can store. Unlike iPhones, Blackberries and personal computers, you cannot add new memory chips to a GPS device. Some of the more expensive devices, however, are capable of accepting memory cards on which data can be stored.

USING A GPS RECEIVER

Left to its own devices, as soon as you switch on a GPS it will begin searching for satellites with which to communicate. But before this can be of meaningful use to you, it is necessary to complete a small set-up procedure, beginning with initialisation.

You first need to get a fix on your current position. To do this, take the device outdoors into a large open area away from buildings and trees. Turn the device on, and keep it face up and parallel with the ground. If it is the first time you have used the device, it will perform a self-test, which is then followed by a satellite page informing you that it is searching for satellites. The device needs to receive strong signals from at least three satellites for it to be able to find your position. When it has done so, you will see a message 'Ready to navigate', and you are now ready to go. However, when you use the device for the first time, it can take up to 5 minutes to find your location; thereafter this should be only a matter of 15–30 seconds. This is because each satellite transmits its own orbital data, known as an 'almanac', and does so every 30 seconds. If the device is left off for some time, the information becomes dated, and so it can take a little time for it to update itself.

You may also need to complete a small set-up routine, just to ensure that the device is functioning correctly for your location. The 'Set-up' screens are under the 'Menu' page, but devices may differ in this regard. Some of the options are obvious, such as time and date. You should set these accordingly. But the only one that is of real concern is on the page called 'Units' – again this may differ from device to device. There are only three entries you need concern yourself with initially. The first is 'Position format'. This relates to the form in which co-ordinate information is relayed to you. For geocaching, this needs to be set at hddd*mm.mmm (see 'A question of degree' box, below). You also need to set the Map Datum to WGS 84 (see 'Understanding co-ordinate systems', below).

Lastly, it is your preference whether the units are expressed as metric or statute – it's just a question of whether you want kilometres and metres or miles and feet. The significance of the position format and datum are explained below.

UNDERSTANDING CO-ORDINATE SYSTEMS

A co-ordinate system is simply a way of describing locations on a map. Across the different countries of the world there are many co-ordinate systems. The British Ordnance Survey, for example, has the grid system, a network of pale blue lines over-printed on maps. This works well in Britain, which is comparatively small. But in larger countries, the curvature of the Earth makes the accuracy of a two-dimensional plan superimposed on what is really a three-dimensional object (the Earth) rather poor. So there are few countries that use this form of grid system. For geocaching purposes, it is simpler to use latitude and longitude, the oldest of the map co-ordinate systems.

A NETWORK OF LINES

Lines of **latitude** run horizontally around the Earth, parallel to the equator (think 'lat' = 'flat', or latitude = around the Earth). These lines measure distances north or south of the equator, and will be your north/south co-ordinates.

As you go north or south from the equator, so the latitude increases from 0° to 90° as you arrive at the poles.

Lines of **longitude** run vertically up the Earth, connecting the north and south poles (think 'long' = 'long lines', or longitude = over the poles). These lines measure the distance, east or west, of the prime meridian at Greenwich in London, England, and these will be your east/west co-ordinates.

When you travel east or west from the prime meridian, the longitude increases from 0° to 180°. The place where the two 180° lines of longitude meet (roughly in the middle of the Pacific Ocean) is known as the International Date Line.

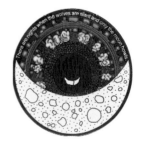

If you are simply out for a walk in the British countryside, then the OS grid system is perfectly adequate; a six-figure grid reference is sufficient to show a location on a map, and, with appropriate map-reading skills, you can use map and compass to walk to that location. But for purposes of geocaching it is generally accepted that the use of latitude and longitude is the norm, and this is the principal system used on www.geocaching.com. It is also the system needed if you are geocaching outside the UK.

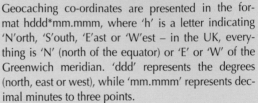

A QUESTION OF DEGREE

Geocaching co-ordinates are presented in the format hddd*mm.mmm, where 'h' is a letter indicating 'N'orth, 'S'outh, 'E'ast or 'W'est – in the UK, everything is 'N' (north of the equator) or 'E' or 'W' of the Greenwich meridian. 'ddd' represents the degrees (north, east or west), while 'mm.mmm' represents decimal minutes to three points.

One degree of latitude is a significant distance, around 70 miles. However, one degree of longitude decreases to zero miles as you head north or south from the equator to the poles. In the UK it ranges from 35 to 44 miles.

A degree is composed of 60 minutes, so a minute of latitude is about 1.2 miles, and a minute of longitude 0.6–0.7 miles.

If all that seems confusing, then you can totally ignore it. All you need to understand is that by this system you can pinpoint a particular location very accurately. Co-ordinates, expressed as numbers, will look like this –

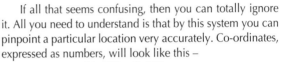

N   53°   42.660
W   002° 38.914

– which is one of the author's caches. This is expressed in degrees and decimal minutes. But over the years, other formats have been devised using either degrees, minutes and seconds (N 53° 42'39" W 002° 38'54") or decimal degrees (N 53.7110 W 002.6486). All three sets of co-ordinates are for the same cache, which shows how confusing things can become, and why it is important to set your GPS device to hddd*mm.mmm, which is what all geocachers use. (The three sets of co-ordinates given above differ because – in the first set, the minutes are decimalised; in the third set, the degrees are decimalised; and the second set doesn't decimalise anything.)

For basic cache searches, you don't need to understand the significance of this information, nor do you need the alternative formats. But, as you will see in another chapter, for some of the more tricky caches you need to understand degrees and decimal minutes well enough to be able to input the data for yourself.

UNDERSTANDING DATUMS

For reasons that are complex and confusing to a lay person, there is no one agreed latitude and longitude co-ordinate system. There are many different meridians of zero longitude (prime meridians) and circles of zero latitude (equators), although the former generally pass somewhere near Greenwich, and the latter is always somewhere near the rotational equator. Different countries base their maps on different mathematical models and on projections representing the shape of the Earth's surface, which, contrary to popular belief, is not a perfect orb but an ellipsoid (flattened at the poles). Each different model is known as a map datum, and many of the world's datums are already programmed into GPS devices.

The result of this mish-mash of information is that different systems of latitude and longitude can disagree on the co-ordinates of any given point by more than 200m. For any application where an error of this size would be significant – docking with a space station, for example – it's important to know which system is being used and exactly how it is defined. Fortunately, for geocaching purposes, the system is simplified; everyone uses the World Geodetic System 1984, known as WGS84, and this is the datum you should select when setting up your GPS device. Should you subsequently want to switch to using the British grid system, then you will need to change the datum to British Grid.

Detailed (and complex) explanations of modern GPS systems are available on the www.ordnancesurvey.co.uk website.

Popular geographical locations are ideal places to conceal and look for caches – and avoiding muggles is part of the fun (photo: Mark Fishwick)

The hedgerow margins along Britain's farm fields
make perfect locations for geocaches

3 GETTING STARTED

The beauty of geocaching is that, compared to many other leisure pursuits, it need not be inordinately expensive. Of course, to start, you do need certain basic items of equipment, not least a GPS receiver. You could manage without a GPS, but your scope for finding caches will be limited and the process more time consuming, and unless you are exceptionally gifted at navigation with map and compass it is more satisfying to invest in a GPS device.

The basic items you need, then, are your GPS device, a map of the area you are in, and the co-ordinates of the caches you are searching for. Chapter 2 deals with various aspects of GPS devices and software for use on an iPhone or Blackberry. There are advantages and disadvantages to each, but it is a good idea to start with an inexpensive GPS device, get the hang of what you're doing, and then decide whether you need to buy something more up-market or investigate how to use your mobile phone for geocaching.

USING WWW.GEOCACHING.COM

The key website to geocaching is www.geocaching.com. Although there are other websites that provide cache co-ordinates (such as www.opencaching.org.uk – see Chapter 10), www.geocaching.com is the main one.

When you first connect with the website it looks a little bewildering, but the more you use it, the clearer things become. The layout of the website may change in future years, but it will contain all the same essential information. What is immediately obvious is that it is very much US oriented, so you need to allow for this. The site www.opencaching.org.uk gets round this issue, but has very few caches in its database at the time of writing (October 2010).

CREATING A MEMBERSHIP

The first thing you need to do is to create a membership.

There are two levels of membership – basic and premium. Basic membership is free; premium membership has a fairly nominal annual or quarterly subscription. At first you may not understand the significance of the differences between the two levels of membership. Suffice to say that the basic membership is just that, basic, allowing you to

download co-ordinates and location information for caches, and to share your experiences online. This is all you need in order to make a start, so it is advisable to opt for this level of membership initially.

However, it will soon become apparent that this option is very limited, and you will find yourself opting for premium membership. Be aware that some caches are available only to premium members, so if you elect to have basic membership you will not find all the caches.

More information about the benefits of premium membership is given in Chapter 9.

MAKE A NAME FOR YOURSELF

Part of the process of creating a membership is deciding on a 'name' for yourself. All the obvious ones – cachebuster, cachemaster, cache machine, cache register, and so on – have long since gone. So you need to invent a pseudonym for yourself that is, perhaps, a composite of initials or names, such as PamandFred, Meandthedog, LostnWet, or something that has significance to you. The author uses 'countrymatters' because, in addition to being a writer of guidebooks about geocaching, he is also a travel journalist to whom countries matter, and an outdoor writer and photographer for whom the country[side] matters. You get the drift? And, yes, he does know to what Shakespeare was referring in *Hamlet* when he mentions 'country matters'.

If you subsequently decide that you want to change your geocaching pseudonym, then you can contact Groundspeak and ask for your name to be changed. This will automatically be transferred to all your log entries, all your finds and all your own caches.

VALIDATION

Having devised a name and created a membership, you are almost ready to go. Part of the membership creation process requires you to validate the email address you are using. So, once you have selected your pseudonym and agreed to the terms and conditions under which geocaching operates, you will be sent an email asking you to validate that the email address really is yours. Once this is done, you can then log in to www.geocaching.com.

ADDING YOUR HOME CO-ORDINATES

Once you have created your membership it is a wise move to add your home co-ordinates. This enables the website database to send you information about caches near you.

Calculating your home co-ordinates can be done either by using your GPS device – it is a good idea to do this

outside your home, assuming it is not surrounded by high-rise buildings that will obstruct a satellite signal – or by asking the website to do it for you.

Log in to the website, and select 'Your profile' (top right panel or left-hand menu). At first you have an almost blank profile screen, but on the right is a small panel headed 'Search options', with a message saying 'You have not selected your home co-ordinates'. This is followed by the option to 'Add them now'. Select this, and you are taken through to a screen showing a map headed 'Manage location'. Now you can see how US-oriented the website is – the map is of a US location.

Try entering your post code (including the space) into the 'Search' field, and click on the 'Search' button. If your post code does not conflict with a similar code in another country, you are then taken through to another map with a small panel on it pointing to a man icon at your post code location. However, because UK post codes cover more than one property, the icon may not correspond exactly with your home address. For complete accuracy simply drag the icon to the correct position on the map, and make a note of the latitude and longitude co-ordinates now showing both on the icon and in the 'Search' field above it. Then select 'Save changes'. You have now told the website where you are.

UNDERSTANDING CACHE PAGES

Select one of the caches from your list, and click on the cache's name to be taken to the detailed 'Cache page'. The screenshots on the following pages show the top and bottom of a typical cache page. There is a lot of information on cache pages, so it is worth ensuring that you understand it. Much of the information also in the table that you get when you search the website for geocaches (see 'Querying the database' below), but there is so much more detail here, and it is this page with which you need to become familiar.

Geocache code and name

A unique 'GC' code (automatically generated by the website) for each cache is shown at the top right of the cache page – GC1Q5P5 in this case. The name – 'Cuerden Valley Park: Stepping Stones' – appears in bold type at the top centre of the page. To the left of the name appears an icon that tells you what type of cache it is (see Chapter 4 for more information).

Cache owner

The name of the person who placed the cache, known as the 'owner', appears immediately below the name of the

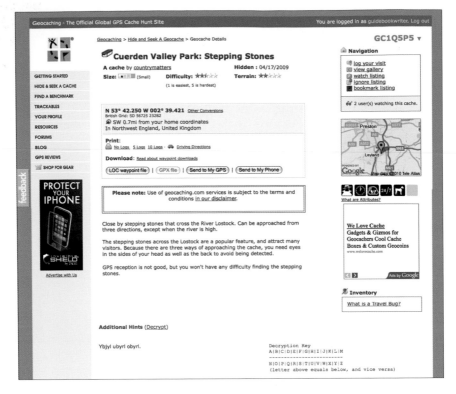

An example of a cache page (top half)

cache, alongside the date on which it was hidden. The name is a pseudonym – in other words, the owner's www.geocaching.com username. If you click on the name, in this case 'countrymatters', you are taken to a page which gives more information about the cache owner. This is their profile page; you will have a similar page, which you can edit.

Cache size

Immediately below the cache owner's name a small grey panel gives an indication of the size of cache container you are looking for. The options are 'micro', 'small', 'regular', 'large' and 'other'. The last category may have further details in the information section below. There is a sub-division of 'micro', which may appear only in the cache description, and this is 'nano'. Nanos are very small and very hard to spot – they tend to be black and magnetic.

For many years, it was the norm to have cache containers that were 'regular' in size – Tupperware boxes and the like. Then, as the activity developed, a range of purpose-made cache containers appeared, among which were some that were very small, some well camouflaged, and some very devious. But all of them made the pursuit all the more enjoyable.

Difficulty and terrain

Alongside the Size panel are two indicators that tell you about the 'difficulty' you might experience in finding the cache, and the nature and condition of the 'terrain' you will encounter. In this context, 1 is easiest, while 5 is the hardest, and the grades are sub-divided into halves. This information is often presented together in the form '1/1' (difficulty/terrain) – this example would therefore be presented as 2.5/2. In total there are 81 possible combinations, about which more is explained in Chapter 10 – for some geocachers it becomes a challenge in itself to find caches of every level. However, while the 'terrain' grade is a fairly clear indicator of what to expect, the 'difficulty' grade may refer to either the actual difficulty of spotting and retrieving the cache, or to the fact that you may have to solve a complex puzzle to discover the co-ordinates. Grading is entirely subjective (see also Chapter 7), and the cache creator designates the level.

Cache co-ordinates

Moving down the cache page, you reach a panel giving location information. This is in three parts

- the first is the latitude and longitude co-ordinates
- the second is the same information expressed in the British grid format
- and the third tells you how far the cache is located from your home co-ordinates.

It is important to remember that latitude and longitude use the WGS84 datum (see Chapter 2), while the British grid datum uses, as the name implies, the British Grid system. You can use either datum, but must ensure that your GPS receiver is set to the appropriate datum.

Printed information

The next option on the cache page is to print a copy of the cache page information, with a choice to include no log entries made by other finders, or 5 or 10 logs. You can even ask the website to give you information about how you can drive from your home co-ordinates to the cache. However, this, while useful in some situations, does need treating with a measure of caution, since it is not possible to drive to many cache locations (because they are up mountains or in the middle of fields, for example). Moreover, you are likely to know your own locality better than www.geocaching.com. So use this option as a guide, but no more. Cache locations to which you can drive and park momentarily are known as 'drive-by' caches or 'cache and dash'.

Co-ordinate downloads

With the exception of low-end GPS devices, it is possible to use an interface cable that allows you to connect your GPS to your computer and directly download co-ordinate information. Called 'paperless geocaching', this works especially well with geocaching-friendly GPS devices, which also allow you to download associated co-ordinates, such as the location of convenient car parks or relevant landmarks. To use this option, you will need to have downloaded software called **Garmin Communicator**, which is simply the means by which the website can 'talk' to your GPS device. The software is downloaded from www8.garmin.com/products/communicator, and comes in PC and Mac versions. Of course, in the UK this works only with Garmin devices, and is not supported by all browsers.

Once the software is installed on your computer, you simply connect your GPS device and click on 'Send to GPS'. This then stores the information in your GPS, ready for you to retrieve.

Description of the cache

Cache descriptions range from brief notes to quite extended descriptions about the cache locality, local history, the geology and geography of the surrounding countryside, and the environment in which it is located. Often there are clues within the description, so it is important to read all the information carefully.

Some cache descriptions also include images, artwork or code, and, quite often, a note about satellite reception if it is particularly variable at the cache location.

A little further down the page is a pale yellow box in which you are able to make notes to yourself that will help you if you are compiling lists of similar caches to search for, or for adding comments from other geocaches as a reminder.

Keep a notebook in which you write down the code and name of the cache(s) you are looking for, along with the clue – deciphered or not according to what you decide. You can always leave the clue encoded, and then decipher it only if you need to.

Additional hints

The cache page itself is a rich source of information and may include an encrypted hint from the cache owner (although not all caches have or need them). Previous finders may have uploaded photos or included clues in their online log. Be careful, though; too much information may inadvertently ruin the fun for you.

The encrypted hints use a simple code format known as the half-reversed alphabet, which looks like this.

A B C D E F G H I J K L M
N O P Q R S T U V W X Y Z

It is easy enough to decipher, as it involves simple transposition (reading either up or down to find the

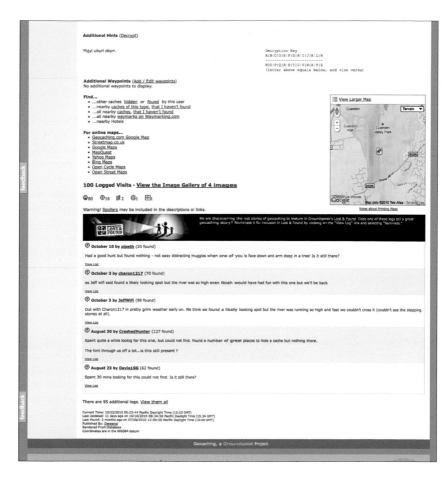

An example of a cache page (bottom half)

corresponding letter) – the word GEOCACHE, for example, translates as TRBPNPUR. But www.geocaching.com has a decryption option anyway. All you need to do is click on 'Decrypt', and it is done instantly.

But you have to make a decision about these clues. Do you use them, or not? They usually give very clear guidance on where to locate the cache, such as 'under a fence' or 'next to an old pipe'. Do you want that level of information? Or do you want to try without it first? Only you can decide, but it is worth remembering that some caches would never be found without the clue, and, to be honest, even with the clue some remain elusive.

Additional waypoints

Under the section headed 'Additional waypoints' you may find information about where to park, about waypoints that will guide you to the cache location, or about other

waypoints that you must visit in order to gather all the information needed to help you to determine the cache co-ordinates.

Find

The 'Find' option has a number of links to

- other caches placed or found by the same owner as the cache you are currently looking for
- nearby caches of the same type (such as traditional caches) that you have yet to find
- all nearby caches you have yet to find regardless of type
- all waymarks listed on www.waymarking.com, about which there is more information in Chapter 10.

Online maps

If you are a premium member of www.geocaching.com, then when you open a cache page on the website you will find links to a number of online maps

- Google Maps
- Geocaching.com Google Map
- Streetmap.co.uk
- MapQuest
- Yahoo Maps
- Bing Maps
- Open Cycle Maps
- Open Street Maps.

The most useful of these are the first three; the others are simply variations on a theme. So, let's take a look at these.

Typical Google map

- **Google Maps** provides a basic map of the area showing the approximate location of the cache, marked by a red symbol. This is not sufficient to get you close, but it will give you an idea of the direction and general area.
- The more detailed www.geocaching.com **Google Map** shows not only the cache you were looking at, but all others nearby, making this the most useful tool for locating caches in any given area. This map also uses different icons to denote the type of cache. With these maps you get an overview of a particular area, and can plan a campaign of cache retrieval based on this. Significantly, once you have logged online that you have found a cache, then the icon on the map changes to show that. It avoids your having to search for caches you have already found.
- www.streetmap.co.uk shows the location of a cache identified by an arrow on an Ordnance Survey Landranger map. This gives you a good idea of the locality you need to get to, and is very useful in pre-planning.

Logged visits

The bottom part of the cache page is where you find everyone's log entries. These are briefly summarised in the following way (see box below).

 58 = found

 2 = not found

 2 = notes, posted by the cache owner, or other geocachers

 1 = the original entry/entries made by the cache reviewer – see Chapter 7

More detailed log entries are then given, ranging from simple notes to extended entries about the experience of finding the cache. Some of the entries have images linked to them, which occasionally reveal information about the cache location. These are known as 'spoilers' for obvious reasons. Whether you use them is for you to decide.

Navigation

At the top right of the cache page, below the cache code, is a Navigation panel. Most of this is for the cache owner to use in order to edit, archive or temporarily disable caches, or to upload images. But it is to this panel that you will ultimately return to log your find (see Chapter 6).

Map location of geocache

Below the Navigation panel there is a small map showing the general area where the cache is located.

A larger map, containing more detail, appears as you scroll down the page. If you click on this larger map, it takes you through to the Geocaching Map for the actual location, and also shows other nearby caches.

Watchers

In the Navigation panel there is an option to 'Watch listing'. This can be used in a number of ways, some of which are explained in later chapters, but essentially it is a way of tracking activity in relation to a particular cache. This option is normally used when you may have failed to find a cache, and want to monitor it to see whether you simply were not diligent enough or whether it has gone missing.

Attributes

Under the map are symbols used to denote the cache's 'attributes', and these tell you what to expect at a cache

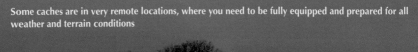
Some caches are in very remote locations, where you need to be fully equipped and prepared for all weather and terrain conditions

location. Cache owners can assign attributes to their cache to indicate

- **permissions** – including whether dogs are allowed
- **conditions** – whether there is a significant amount of walking involved, the route is suitable for children, the cache available at all times, and so on
- **special equipment** – whether there is a parking fee, or the need for a torch or climbing equipment
- **hazards** – such as thorns or dangerous terrain
- **facilities** – including accessibility for wheelchairs, and availability of parking and public transport.

Premium members can run a search, known as a Pocket Query (see Chapter 9), to search for caches with particular attributes.

Inventory

Chapter 8 gives more information about trackable items, known as travel bugs or geocoins, that may be found in cache containers. Any such trackable items currently located in a cache are listed in the inventory (under the 'Attributes' list).

Left-hand menu
The left-hand menu is largely self-explanatory, but more detailed explanations are given in later chapters at the appropriate point.

QUERYING THE DATABASE
The sensible thing to do first is to find geocaches near your home. This can be done in two ways – these are essentially different website routes to the same end result. On the home page of www.geocaching.com is a section headed 'Search for geocaches'. In this section there are two fields. The first field may contain a number that means nothing to you at this stage. But to the right of the field is a button icon saying 'Locate me'.

1 If your computer is **using WiFi** to connect to the internet, then this button can be used to locate where you are (where you live). Just click on 'Locate me', and the system will do the rest, if it can, and will generate co-ordinates for your home location, and these will be saved in the field. However, this method is not wholly reliable.

The second field contains the initials GC; this relates to caches for which you already have the geocaching code – they all begin with the letters GC. But as you have yet to find a cache, this is something to come back to later.

2 Alternatively, in the first field you can enter your home postcode (with or without spaces), then click on 'Go', and you will be presented with a list of caches near your home and radiating outwards from it for anything up to 40km (25 miles); you'll be surprised how many there are.

However, because of the US bias of the website, entering your post code may not always work, particularly if there are identical or similar post codes elsewhere in the world. If it doesn't work using your post code, then try entering the name of a town near where you live. (Using the name of a village may not be sufficient, but major towns will be found.) When you click on 'Go', a list of caches near to the town will appear.

You can also reach cache information via the left-hand menu option 'Hide and seek a cache', or by using the 'Advanced search' option in the 'Search for geocaches' field on the website home page, both of which allow you a greater choice of fields with which to narrow down your search. If you search for caches restricting your search criteria just to the UK, you will find that there are almost 55,000 of them – reason enough to start narrowing things down.

You can use the option of entering a town name in the search field to find caches located in places away from home that you are visiting, both elsewhere in the UK and abroad.

UNDERSTANDING THE RESULTS

Once you have your list of caches, you can start searching for them. It helps if you can get a visual idea of where they are, and you can do this by using Google Maps. All you do now is to select the caches you want to go out and find. So, turn to the list you have generated; it will look something like this.

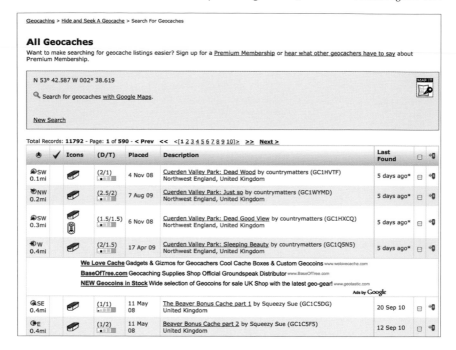

List of geocaches from a given waypoint

But what does it all mean? The first thing to realise is that the table is giving you information about caches concealed at a certain distance from your home co-ordinates. If you now click on 'Search for geocaches with Google Maps' you will receive a display of the cache locations on a map, which is a very useful visual indication both of the caches, and the types of cache (represented by various icons), near you. This facility works for both basic and premium membership levels.

- **Column 1** of the list gives the distance of the cache from your home co-ordinates, with the nearest listed first – in this instance, 0.1 miles south-west, 0.2 miles north-west, 0.3 miles south-west, and so on.

- **Column 2** is blank, but will have a tick placed in it automatically once you've found the cache and recorded your find online. When you start placing caches of your own, this column will also contain an icon to that effect.

- **Column 3** contains icons that tell you what type the cache is. Chapter 4 explains the different cache types, but to begin with choose a cache that looks like a green-topped brick; these are known as 'traditional' caches, the basic type. Occasionally, there are other icons in this column, and these refer to what are known as 'trackable items' that may be in the cache: Chapter 8 explains what these are.
- **Column 4** gives some information about the ease with which the cache might be found and retrieved. The letters 'D/T' indicate 'Difficulty' and 'Terrain' – in other words, how difficult the cache is to find, and how complex the terrain is that you will need to cross to get to it. The numbers (1/1) are the easiest, with (5/5) being (often) inordinately difficult. Also in this column the little grey panel with a red square indicates the approximate size of the cache you are looking for, with the smallest square being on the left-hand side and the largest on the right.
- **Column 5** tells you the date on which the cache was placed.
- **Column 6** gives a brief description of the cache, along with its code name (eg GC1C5F5), which, once you've noted or remembered it, can be used as a quick way of accessing a particular cache via the home page of www.geocaching.com.
- **Column 7** tells you when the cache was last found (and if you have found it, when you did so).
- **Column 8** is a shortcut to downloading cache information to a GPS device. Just click the boxes to select the caches you want to look for. To send the information to your GPS, of course, it first has to be connected to your computer and switched on. If you cannot do this, then you are faced with manually inputting the co-ordinates yourself. This is no real hardship, but the ability to send information to your GPS device does speed things up.
- **Column 9** shows a small icon of a GPS device. This is another way that you can download co-ordinate information from the website to your GPS device. This uses software known as Garmin Communicator, which you can download from the www.geocaching.com website.

The dramatic rock formations of Kilt Rock on the Isle of Skye are perfect examples of the kind of geological structures that underpin the earth science requirements of all EarthCaches

4 SELECTING GEOCACHES TO FIND

To begin with it's a good idea to select a cache close to your home – one you can walk to easily without causing concern to anyone in your family that you are going off into the wilderness in search of buried treasure and may never come back. Once you have found your first cache, then suddenly everything starts to fall into place and make sense. There is also a certain excitement about your first find.

DO YOUR HOMEWORK

Your search adventure begins at home as you query the database and compile your list of possible caches to find, as described in Chapter 3.

It is easiest to begin with a traditional cache (the ones with the green-topped brick icon), so for the moment ignore any of the others.

But before you dash out there are a few other issues to consider.

- Do you intend to go out alone, or with a friend or members of your family?
- Is everyone equally agile – could they cope with stiles and gates, for example?
- Will you be taking a dog along?

Now check the attributes of the cache to see if the cache is in a family-friendly location, or is open to dogs, or open all hours, or involves a significant walk. The attributes enable you to find an easy cache to begin with; one that satisfies your requirements. There are a great many attributes, as you will discover when you start placing caches yourself, but only eight can be displayed.

MAKE USE OF THE SEARCH OPTIONS

An alternative way of locating caches near you is to use the 'Search options' facility on www.geocaching.com.

When you log on to the website, select either 'My profile' in the top right panel on the home page or 'Your profile' from the left-hand menu bar. 'Your profile' lists caches you have found, and these soon start to increase in number. To the right of the list is another panel with a range of options, among which is 'Search options'. The first part of this allows you to search for the geocaches nearest to your home

Once you have found a cache you want to search for, first check the logs entered by other geocachers. These appear at the bottom of the individual cache pages. From these logs you can obtain information that may help you in your search or, more importantly, tell you whether the cache is missing. Each log entry gives the date on which the cache was found. If you encounter a run of entries indicating that the cache was not found, then it may well have been lost or removed.

These tree roots, which conceal a 2/2.5 cache, can prove slippery to the unwary

Remember, caches are concealed, not buried. You won't have to go armed with a spade to dig things up, but you may have to get into some muddy or awkward situations.

co-ordinates – of course, this presupposes that you have entered your home co-ordinates (see Chapter 3).

GATHERING CACHE INFORMATION

As you decide on a geocache you want to look for, keep in mind the following.

- Have you considered the **difficulty** and **terrain ratings** of the cache? It makes sense to choose a 1/1 difficulty and terrain rating for your first geocache find so that you can learn how geocaches are placed. But 1/1 really is very easy, and (perhaps surprisingly) there may not be many of them, or any near your home. For a first search, you could realistically tackle anything up to a 2.5/2.5.
- Consult the **maps** of the area. Is this an urban or rural cache? And how might this change your planning? Road maps may be adequate in a town or city, but topographical maps, such as the Ordnance Survey Explorer or Landranger series, and the specialist maps produced by Harvey Maps, all of which show land and water features, may be more useful elsewhere. The OS Explorer and Harvey's maps tell you what terrain you will encounter, while the former also give an indication of what is known as 'Access Land', where you may roam freely.
- Keep in mind that **distances** can be deceiving. Understand the difference between distances in a direct line and the actual distance of travel. You could be metres from a cache according to your GPS device, but

there might be a river or other obstacle in the way. Part of the fun is that you have to find the best route to a cache, and usually it is not direct.

- Once you are close to the cache location, you can **navigate** using your GPS device. For instance, if you are in a small park, you can try to simply follow the GPS arrow. In a large park, this method might be challenging, so follow the established trails as much as possible while still keeping the GPS arrow heading the general direction of the cache location.

Preparation and research will vary for each cache. Many geocachers find that they begin with online maps to get an idea of the area, and then decide to supplement this with a detailed paper map.

If you plan to tackle a sequence of caches, mark these on a paper map, so that you can more easily plan a route between them. But beware – while a mile of walking may take 20 minutes or so, a mile of geocaching can easily take double the time.

TYPES OF CACHE

There is a potentially bewildering range of caches, some with a number of variations on a theme, and some that have been discontinued.

Traditional cache

This is the most common and most basic of caches – a simple container with a logbook in it. Typically these are Tupperware-like plastic boxes that can be locked, but containers that once held 35mm film are increasingly being used. Less commonly, caches take the form of old ammunition boxes or buckets. For a traditional cache, the co-ordinates given on the cache page give the location of the cache (but see 'A question of accuracy', below).

This 3/4.5 EarthCache is a long way out on desolate moorland. Are you properly equipped?

Multi-cache

A multi- (or multiple) cache may well take the physical form of a traditional cache, but it will involve two or more locations from which you obtain information, contained in the cache container, that leads to the final cache location. There are a number of variations in this group. Some multi-caches simply form a trail to follow – they contain a hint or co-ordinates that will guide you to another cache, and so on until you reach the final cache. Others contain letters or numbers which, having gained all of them from successive caches, are used to calculate the co-ordinates of the final, bonus cache. the most demanding of this type is arguably GC154N9 which involves visiting every county in England!

Offset cache

Caches that require you to go to a location and get hints to the co-ordinates – such as dates on a monument – of the actual cache are known as offset caches. Caches typical of this type provide information that enables you to complete, for example, the co-ordinates

    N   54°   AB.CDE
    W 002° FG.HIJ

There are many variations on this theme. At the most basic you pick up one letter/number at each of ten traditional caches, with those numbers completing the co-ordinates of the final, bonus cache. Other formats may take you to, say, only four caches, and then tell you that A+B=G, C-A=J, D÷B=F, and so on. The permutations are virtually endless. In this sort of format it is not unusual for the figures for degrees to be provided, eg N 54° and W 002°, because these will be fairly constant for your local area.

Mystery and puzzle caches

As the name suggests, these caches are for the dedicated puzzler, those who love to wrestle with code breaking, cryptic clues, cyphers, origami, and so on. It can take a long time to decypher some of the co-ordinate information. So you either have to rise to the challenge or stick to straightforward, uncomplicated caches.

Typical examples of puzzles might involve using a particular font from a conventional computer, such as

Others may use a simple substitution code –

A	B	C	D	E	F	G	H	I	J
1	2	3	4	5	6	7	8	9	0

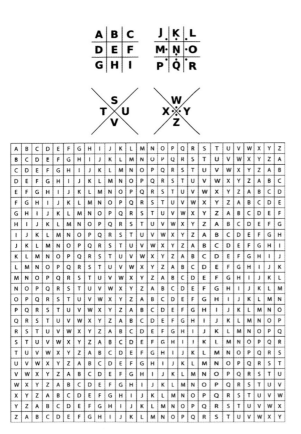

Other code examples:
Pigpen cypher (top) and
Vigènere cypher (bottom)

But the more complicated puzzle caches use a bewildering variety of cyphers and codes ranging from bar codes (GCNKD3), matrix or binary codes (GC1RM4W), the Pigpen cypher (also known as the Masonic cypher, and used by Dan Brown in his book *The Lost Symbol*) (GC1WYDR), and the textura dextra, or Vigènere, cypher (GC1QB55). Some use combinations of two or more codes. All of these are infuriatingly difficult and time-consuming to crack, but provide endless pre-occupation for those who like a challenge.

To make matters worse, the creativity ingenuity of some geocachers is making this type of cache both popular and increasingly complex. For evidence of this, take a look at GCP5MD and GCJRQ1. In short, you can expect problems and hours of puzzlement every time you encounter a cache with a difficulty rating of 4.5 or 5.

Letterbox-hybrid cache

Letterboxing was a forerunner of geocaching. In this format, you were given clues instead of co-ordinates to locate a pot (the letterbox) containing a rubber stamp and a visitors' book. More recently letterbox hybrids have evolved, which are a combination of conventional geocaching co-ordinates posted on the website and a cache that contains a rubber stamp, which you can use to record your visit. In practice, this means that if you are searching for letterbox-hybrid caches, you will need to carry a small inkpad for use with the stamp. The stamp must remain in the cache, but an inkpad would dry out quickly and become unusable.

EarthCaches

An EarthCache does not have a physical cache container. EarthCaches are special places that you can visit to learn about a particular aspect of Earth science. EarthCache pages contain the usual co-ordinate information, but also have extended notes on the significance of the cache location. EarthCaches are intended to convey an educational aspect that enables visitors to see how the Earth has been shaped by geological processes (see GC2D6AM).

Visiting EarthCaches is an enjoyable experience for all the family, and participants are relieved of the responsibility of trying to find a concealed cache. You can identify EarthCaches near you by using the 'EarthCache listings' option on www.earthcache.org.

When you do arrive at an EarthCache location, you will need to take certain action to confirm that you were there. This could range from taking a photograph of yourself at the location (although this is no longer obligatory), to answering a series of question relevant to the site (see 'Creating an EarthCache' in Chapter 7).

Event caches

From time to time groups of geocachers get together to organise a social event, ranging from an evening meal in a pub to an organised outing searching collectively for caches. These might coincide with dates such as the summer solstice, historical events, New Year's Day, and so on, and they are simply a medium for local and regional geocachers to get together and socialise. Because the event is a cache in itself, attendance gains you a point score in your overall tally of caches found. But shortly afterwards the event the cache is archived. So you have to be quick! Large gatherings of this type are known as 'mega-event caches', attended by at least 500 geocachers, but fundamentally the principles are the same.

Grandfathered caches

The expression 'grandfathered' relates to cache types that are no longer available for creation, but which still exist to be found. Examples of these are as follows.

- **Virtual caches** – this type of cache exists only in the form of a location (there is no physical cache), but it is one that you have to visit. Once at the site of a virtual cache, you will have to answer a question about the location, or about someone who lived or worked nearby. The 'reward' for these caches is the actual location, and then sharing information about your visit. GCE387 is a classic example – the Palace of Westminster in London, otherwise known as the Houses of Parliament and Big Ben.

- **Webcam caches** – this interesting form of cache is difficult to complete because it involves someone else in addition to yourself. Across the country there are a number of places where webcams have been positioned. What you have to do is get yourself in front of the camera in order to record your visit. But the difficult bit is that you need someone to sit a computer, logged on to www.geocaching.com and to the cache page in particular, to capture the image. The webcam image on the cache page refreshes from time to time, and your task is to get someone to save the image with you in it, to prove that you were there. With the development of mobile broadband and WiFi internet connections, however, it is possible for you to use a hand-held device or small laptop to make the connections yourself as you stand in front of the camera. It is all a little high tech, but good fun.
- **Cuckoo caches** – this type of cache is a travelling cache, a cache within a cache; find one and you find two. Your task is then to take the cuckoo cache to a different cache and leave it there for someone else to find and move on, although this is not obligatory (you can leave it where it is). In many ways it is like a conventional trackable item (see Chapter 8). GC4C35 is a typical example of a cuckoo cache.

THE SIZE OF CACHES

The bigger the cache container the easier (theoretically) it is to find. For some time, before they became militaria collectors' items, old ammunition boxes were used, and while these can still be found, there are few new ones appearing that use this type of container.

Increasingly, geocachers are using lockable plastic containers available from supermarkets, although it is possible to buy geocaching-specific boxes from a number of online sources – but see also Chapter 7.

The cache page gives information near the top of the size of the cache you are looking for, and this should be noted.

A webcam cache in the village of Coniston – notice the camera to the left of the left-hand chimney. These caches are no longer permitted as 'new' caches, but most of the old ones remain active

A QUESTION OF ACCURACY

You might think that if you are armed with cache co-ordinates you can walk straight up to a cache location, and sometimes this is the case. But more often you will find that the co-ordinates appear to be slightly inaccurate. There are reasons for this which are partly to do with inconsistencies in information transmitted by satellites (see Chapter 2). But more often the inaccuracies are related to factors that can restrict 'satellite view' and so give less than spot-on readings, such as trees, overhanging cliffs and tall buildings. The cache owner will have tried to get the best possible reading, but it may not correspond exactly with the location of the cache. More to the point, there is a skill in recording co-ordinate information (see Chapter 7), and if the original cache owner does not have that skill, then the co-ordinates themselves may be inaccurate. See 'Adding a waypoint' in Chapter 6 to learn what to do about this.

GOOGLE EARTH

The basic version of Google Earth is downloadable free from www.google.com and provides high-resolution satellite images of the Earth. With a bit of practice you can zoom in to the locality of your cache search, get some idea of the terrain, and even place a marker at the exact co-ordinates of the cache. The detail is outstanding.

The Google Earth image is also useful in planning how you might approach a cache location, and what obstacles you might encounter. Of course, tree cover conceals everything, but as a guide Google Earth has much to commend it.

Section taken from Google Earth

SELECTING GEOCACHES TO FIND

Checking your location using map and compass is a useful skill in geocaching

5 SEARCHING FOR A GEOCACHE

At a basic level, searching for a geocache involves no more than storing the cache co-ordinates in a GPS device, and then going out to find it, using the GPS alone. But it is rarely as simple as that.

Even so, this is where the fun begins, and the satisfaction of finding caches never abates. Find 10, and you want to make it 20, then 50 and 100, 200, 300, 1000. With over 1 million caches worldwide, you won't run out.

MAP AND COMPASS TECHNIQUES
The ability to use a map and compass, while not critical, does help in the search for geocaches. At the very least, being able to understand and read a topographic map (such as an Ordnance Survey map) does enable you to get an approximate fix on the location of a cache and to assess what obstacles might lie in the way. Using a map such as this enables you to plan a route to link caches and to navigate around unexpected obstacles such as rivers, buildings, steep ground and woodland.

For a detailed exposition of map and compass techniques, you might usefully consult *Map and Compass: The Art of Navigation* by Pete Hawkins (Cicerone Press, 2003) or the author's own *Map Reading Skills* (Crimson Publishing, 2007). Both explain at some length how to acquire and develop the skills of navigation.

WHAT TO TAKE WITH YOU
In deciding what to take with you, much will depend on how many caches you are hoping to find, what distance lies between them, and how long you plan to be out. If you are making a day of it, then a map, compass, GPS and suitable clothing and footwear are all obvious items to take. In this respect, geocaching is no different from going out for a walk (although it will be more time consuming) and you should be appropriately equipped – you may spend a good deal of time relatively inactive and getting cold. It is useful, too, to print out the cache information from the website.

You will also need a pen to sign logbooks; many caches already contain pens and/or pencils, but this cannot be guaranteed. So get into the habit of taking your own, and preferably one that is waterproof – logbook pages are often damp.

Other items that have been found useful include a

- pair of tweezers (for extracting rolled up logs from small cache containers)
- pocket knife (to help open some of the more difficult containers and sharpen pencils)
- torch and spare batteries (to check the insides of pipes, for example, or to search in poorly lit locations, such as among tree roots or down holes)
- pair of gloves (to protect hands against caches concealed in prickly or stinging locations, and to search in holes that might be occupied – we do have adders in the UK, and they do not like to be disturbed)
- walking stick or pole (with which to poke about in holes or bushes).

It is also good practice and courteous to carry a few small plastic bags, which can be used to protect caches that may have become wet or damaged, and even a small notebook in case you find the existing logbook full. If either of these possibilities are encountered, you have the option, when logging your find on www.geocaching.com, to leave a 'maintenance' note for the owner, explaining what is necessary and what you have done as an interim measure.

You may also have 'travellers' – travel bugs and geocoins (see Chapter 8) – that you want to take, or items that you want to leave in the cache. Occasionally you may be asked to take a photograph of yourself or a location to prove that you were there. So that means a camera, too, although the images produced by many mobile phones are perfectly adequate for geocaching purposes.

Gnomes from home – someone has created a small cache shelter for these guardian gnomes, and caches like this are always a favourite with children

SOME COURTESY AND SAFETY CONSIDERATIONS

Although geocaching should be no more hazardous a pastime than recreational walking, there are a few additional considerations.

- **Be aware of your responsibilities** as a walker and observe the Countryside Code (www.naturalengland.org.uk).
- **Consider taking someone with you**, especially if you are going into remote or difficult terrain.
- **Leave a note** in a conspicuous place in your car to say where you are going, possibly giving the cache co-ordinates; that way, if you become lost people will know where to look for you. It is a debateable issue whether you give an indication of the expected time of return, as this simply tells thieves how long they have to break into your car. In any case, you will take much longer than you think!
- **Take something to eat and drink.**
- Before you go, **check the weather forecast**, then, while out on the search, keep an eye on the sky and pay attention to the passage of time.
- During the grouse-shooting season or periods of deer stalking, **check with the relevant estates** that it is safe for you to go, and, if necessary, be prepared to change your plans.
- **Do not touch discarded items** – they could be hazardous.
- Do not forget to **look up from your GPS from time to time** to avoid walking over cliff edges or into ditches, and to spot potholes, overhanging branches or other obstructions.

SEARCH STRATEGIES

Once you move on beyond searching for single caches to a series, it makes sense to have a basic strategy and technique. Everyone does this in a different way, and you may well devise your own. But here is a basic strategy to use as a starting point.

- Begin by **plotting the cache locations on a map**. If you look at the cache page, then you will see that beneath the co-ordinates in latitude and longitude the location is given in terms of the British Grid system. This allows you to roughly pinpoint the location on a map. You can also check with www.streetmap.co.uk to be sure you have the location approximately correct.
- Now **study the map** and figure out how you can legally link all the caches together in one circular walk (assuming you want to get back to your starting point). In

SEARCHING FOR A GEOCACHE

Geocaches are to be found throughout the UK, including in the countryside, where geocaching offers a great alternative to crowded beaches (photo: Mark Fishwick)

this context, and if the caches are in the countryside, Ordnance Survey maps at 1:25,000 scale show Access Land, which is areas of land, usually upland or moorland, that you can wander freely across without having to stay on public rights of way. However, it is worth remembering that footpaths evolved where they did for a reason, and that reason may well be the difficulty of the ground to either side of it. Wandering freely isn't always a good idea.

- **Download the co-ordinates** to your GPS device and check that they are there. Note, however, that your GPS will show only those caches that are close to the current GPS location – for example, your home. If you are in the UK and download co-ordinates for caches in, say, France, then they will not be displayed on the GPS until the device has actually located your position in France. But beware! Remember to delete your French caches before you return home, as once you are back in the UK they will remain on your device but won't be displayed, and thus take up limited GPS memory.

- If you have not printed out the cache information, then at least **carry a small notebook**, and in it enter the cache code (GC??????), its name (because often there is a clue in the name), and, if you want to do this, then decrypt the clue and write that information in your notebook, too. Or at least enter the encrypted string of characters with a view to decrypting them later, out in the field, should you have difficulty finding the cache.

- Check that you have **spare batteries** for your GPS.
- When you get to your starting point, **check** with the map **that you are following the correct route**. You can enter key landmark features – such as bridges and road junctions – into your GPS as waypoints, and use these to navigate along the route. But remember that if you use only cache co-ordinates, then the GPS device will show only straight line connections. It may not be possible to walk in a straight line.

GETTING CLOSE

Your GPS device will get you fairly close to the cache location, but bear in mind that accuracy is a rather vague notion affected not least by the disposition of satellites and the skill of the cache owner in taking the original readings when the cache was put in place. Some GPS devices will emit an audible signal as you approach the cache co-ordinates ('ground zero' or 'GZ'), but it is rare that the co-ordinates and the actual location coincide precisely. Now is the moment to put your own skills to the test.

- Begin by thinking about the **cache container**. The cache page tells you whether this is large or small, and some give even more information – such as whether it is an ammunition box, film container, cigar case, etc. So, an ammunition box is not going to be concealed in a narrow fissure in a rock.
- Many **cache containers are camouflaged** so that they blend in with the background. But what you are looking for is a shape that does not belong in a natural landscape. The more geocaching you do, the more you will learn to recognise what is natural and what is not – straight lines and perfect circles rarely occur in nature.
- Once you arrive at the cache co-ordinates, take a moment to **scan the terrain** rather than moving haphazardly across it. Look at the lie of the land, trying to figure out what would make a good hiding place. Bearing in mind that caches are concealed, not buried, some popular hiding places are cracks in rocks, the base of trees, tree stumps, fallen logs, natural hollows and piles of rocks. Microcaches, however, are a major challenge to anyone's observational skills and patience. By their nature these are small objects in a large space, and spotting them is not easy, but it is rewarding when you achieve it.

The spectacular geology along the ascent of Ingleborough from Crina Bottom is ideal for the creation of an EarthCache

- While searching for a cache you need to be constantly on the look-out for **anything that looks unnatural**: 'organised' piles of twigs and branches ('stickoflage', for want of a better expression), groups of stones that look just a little too tidy, or piles of rocks that have a different colouration from the surrounding rocks. As time goes by, you learn to spot these differences from a distance.
- When you reach the cache location ask yourself **where would you conceal a cache** – look there first. Trusting intuition is something all geocachers do. Begin by checking the obvious hiding places.
- If a thorough search of GZ does not reveal the cache, then **widen your search area**, bearing in mind the in-built inaccuracies in location already mentioned. Quite often just a few strides away makes all the difference.

It is worth calibrating the compass on your GPS device whenever it has been idle for more than a few days. There is an option on all devices to do this. Failure to do so could send you round in circles.

THE TROUBLE WITH 'MUGGLES'

As any fan of Harry Potter will understand, a 'muggle' (in geocaching terms) is someone who doesn't geocache. Inevitably, when out geocaching, you will encounter muggles. The trouble with muggles is that they do not know what geocaching is about, and so it is vital to ensure the security of caches by searching for, locating, retrieving and replacing cache containers when there are no muggles about. This can be challenging in itself, especially with caches concealed in town centre parks, along main roads, on housing estates or in shopping centres, for example.

Stealth is all important, and you may have to suspend searching if muggles approach, resuming again once they have passed. Trying to look nonchalant often works, but it is only a small step from looking suspicious; the last thing you want is the sudden appearance of authority enquiring what you are up to.

There are many ways of diverting attention when muggles approach – it is amazing how many geocachers suddenly find the need to re-tie shoelaces, to pick up something that appears to have fallen from a pocket, or who seem to be making a call on a mobile phone that only close inspection shows to be a GPS device. A loud-ish and animated 'phone' conversation is certain to keep passing muggles at bay. Carrying a camera and pretending to take shots of leaves, flowers, lichen or rock formations is another technique.

The reason for all this subterfuge is to make certain that inquisitive muggles do not attempt to see what you were up to after you leave. Each year, caches disappear because they have been 'muggled'. The reasons for this loss range from malicious to unintentional, but every loss is a loss to the pursuit until they are replaced.

A splendid EarthCache: the Giant's Causeway, Northern Ireland

6 DISCOVERING A GEOCACHE

The primary aim of geocaching is to find concealed caches, and to have fun while you're doing it. Simple enough you might think. But what do you have to do when you actually discover a cache? Is there an 'etiquette' to be observed? And what do you do if you are unable to find a cache?

WHAT TO DO WHEN YOU FIND A GEOCACHE

Caches are not going to be in plain view. You may hit on one almost immediately, or you may spend some considerable time hunting around, and trying to look nonchalant while doing so in order not to draw attention to yourself.

Once you have the cache container in your hands, enjoy the moment and the sense of accomplishment that goes with it – this is, after all, something you located and retrieved by your own endeavour. You can feel chuffed – no one's watching!

One of the first things to do is to take a moment to note how, and precisely where, the container was concealed. When you leave the site, you want to replace a cache exactly as it was found. Another key point at this early stage is to take a quick look around to ensure you are not being observed.

Now walk away from the site, with the container in your hand. If it is convenient to do so, perch on a rock or a bench and look as though you are taking a breather or having a bite to eat. Cache containers that really are Tupperware 'lunch' boxes are excellent for this little subterfuge.

OPENING THE CACHE

Depending on the age of the cache, it may be in pristine condition, or it may be grubby or damaged. If it is damaged, there is a good chance that water has penetrated, leaving whatever is in the container in a mess. So, take care opening the container, just in case. If it is filled with water and everything in it sodden, then you need to attempt some kind of repair, although some caches will be beyond redemption. Tip out the water and do your best to make the container dry. Remove any sodden items from the container and take them away for disposal, but leave the log in place, however wet it is – you can send a maintenance message to the cache owner when you log your visit on the website.

If you are searching with children and you are the first to find the cache, consider pretending that you didn't, and then directing one of the children to the spot, so that they discover it. They'll enjoy the experience all the more, and be more willing to try geocaching again.

Because cache containers come in all shapes and sizes, the opening 'mechanism' will vary; some are simple plastic clip locks, others have flip tops, while many of the smaller ones screw together. In recent years, old plastic medicine bottles have started to appear, the kind that have infuriating 'child-proof' tops that only a child can open!

SIGNING THE LOG

Official log book

Each cache contains a record log of some kind. Those that are large enough hold small notebooks, some purpose-made, others improvised. You may also find pencils (for signing the log – don't remove them) and even pencil sharpeners.

The very small cache containers hold a rolled-up or folded strip of paper in place of a notebook. These serve just as well, but can be notoriously difficult to extricate from the cache container.

Always carry a spare 'logbook' to replace any that are found to be full. This is actually the responsibility of the cache owner, but it does no harm – and a lot of good – to ensure that any cache containers you find are properly equipped. There is no need to use a notebook; there are log sheets available on the internet, and these will serve just as well. There is a sample available for download at **www. nwcaching.co.uk/ Media**.

Always carry a pair of tweezers to help extract single-sheet 'logbooks' from the smaller caches, along with a pen that has waterproof ink.

The logbook is a record of everyone who has found the cache. It is interesting to spend a few minutes looking through the log entries, and reading what fun others may have had finding the cache. The more you 'cache' around your local area, the more names you will come to recognise. Many of them you may subsequently meet at a local event cache.

Go to the next available space in the logbook and make your own entry. An absolute minimum is your geocaching name and the date. If you chance to be the first person to find the cache (FTF), then you should enter the time, too. It is an agreeable and considerate part of the pursuit to add a few comments, including the names of any other geocachers who were with you, and to say something about your search for the cache – the weather, the terrain conditions and so on. At the very least, it is courtesy to enter 'TFTC' (Thanks for the cache) and 'TNLN' (Took nothing, left nothing – if that is appropriate) – but see 'Trading', below, and 'Trackable items' in Chapter 8.

Some geocachers have small 'calling cards' printed, with space in which to enter the date, and they leave these in the cache, although it is always a good idea to sign the actual log. Others have rubber stamps made with which to stamp the logbook, or custom-made adhesive labels to fix into the log.

Some cache containers are so small, however, that all you can do is enter the date and your initials. You should not use up space in a small logbook by entering extended messages – keep it simple.

A few caches contain small cameras that visitors are asked to use to take a picture of themselves at the cache site

before replacing the camera. The cache owner makes periodic visits to retrieve the camera, and then posts the pictures on the geocaching website. If you encounter such a cache, you need to be clear that the camera is not a trading item (see below), but should be left in the cache.

The rocks in the foreground of this picture are a perfect site for concealing a cache, but it may still take a while before you actually locate it

TRADING

One of the underlying principles of geocaching is 'trading' – that is, putting some trinket or 'treasure' into a cache and taking something out. Of course, this is possible only with containers large enough to take items, but the basic rule is that you should 'trade up' – in other words, put in something of greater worth than you take out.

In reality, the business of trading up is not always feasible, because each time there is a trade the items put in the cache are (in theory) of higher value, and there is a limit to how far you go – it would take some trading up to replace the wrist watch (still ticking away after four winter months) found in one Lake District cache, or the functioning digital device for measuring map distances found in southern Scotland.

In practice, 'trading up' has evolved into 'swapping' – in other words, put something in, take something out regardless of value. This particular aspect of geocaching is of special appeal to children, who may well find small toys and games in caches. One cache in Lancashire is used by www.bookcrossing.com as a repository for books. Leave behind a book you have read and take another in its place. You need

Sample calling card

countrymatters
found this
cache
24/12/2010
TFTC

DISCOVERING A GEOCACHE

to be registered as a member of Bookcrossing, and you do still need to find the cache containing the books, but it adds another appealing dimension to the pursuit.

If you don't have anything to trade, then the correct thing to do is simply to sign the logbook and take nothing (TNLN). Don't take something without leaving something in its place. The exceptions to this rule are travel bugs and geocoins (see Chapter 8).

As you discover more caches, so you get a better idea of the sort of thing that people leave behind – rarely, if ever, is it anything unsavoury, nor should it be. It can be just about anything that will fit into the cache container – but here are some guidelines.

- **Do not leave food items**, not even sweets – food attracts animals, and some containers have been chewed into or knocked about by foxes and badgers looking for something to eat.
- **Do not leave anything that is illegal, dangerous or potentially offensive** – geocaching is a family activity; be considerate and responsible.
- If you are trading, **try to leave something of at least equal value** – don't, for example, take a small piece of jewellery and leave a plastic toy from a burger bar.
- **Clear out the rubbish** – some caches gradually fill up with trash, broken toys, cheap plastic stuff, battered golf balls, rusting badges and so on, and these should be removed. But also, over time, some items deteriorate in quality. So, as a guide, if the items in the cache are not something you would happily put in your coat pocket, put them in a carrier bag and ditch them in a rubbish bin at the first opportunity. It does no harm and a lot of good to maintain caches in this way, even if they are not your own; there is nothing more disappointing than a cache that is not maintained.
- **Think about what you put in** – is the next visitor likely to find your trade item interesting, useful or fun?

RETURNING THE CACHE CONTAINER

Before you leave the cache location, you must return the container to its original place and conceal it properly. Here are a few tips you might follow in doing so.

- Make a point of checking to **ensure that the container is properly closed** – there is nothing worse than opening a cache container that is full of stagnant water because the previous finder didn't close it properly.
- **Put the cache back where you found it**, concealed at least as well as it was. Because caches occasionally get disturbed and are found in the open, or slightly exposed,

it makes sense, and is good practice, to ensure that the cache is properly hidden. Don't make it more difficult to find, but do make it secure. And remember, one of the give-aways of a cache hiding place is that whatever is covering it does not look natural. Bear this in mind when replacing a cache.

- **Make sure you have left nothing behind** – and that includes lunch wrappers or tissues, as well as your GPS, mobile phone, car keys, camera, dog or children.
- **Cover your tracks** – many caches can be found because previous finders have created a 'Cachers' Path' to them. Do you best to avoid this, and try not to leave any evidence of your visit.

LOGGING YOUR FIND

Part of the fun of geocaching is sharing your experience of finding a cache with others. You do this on the www.geo-caching.com website by finding the cache you have located using any of the methods previously described, although the speediest is simply to enter the GC code on the home page of the website. You can log your find at any time – days, weeks or months after you found it. But it is a good idea to get into the habit of logging the find as soon as you can, so that you don't forget it.

To log a find, go to the Navigation panel on the cache page and select 'Log your visit'. You are redirected to a page headed 'Post a new log' (see screenshot below), on which there are three main fields.

The first is the **'Type of log'** field – the main choices are 'Found it', 'Didn't find it', 'Write a note', 'Needs archiving' and 'Needs maintenance'. So, select 'Found it'.

Other entries in the 'Type of log' field are listed below.

- 'Didn't find it' – you looked for the cache but failed to find it (see 'What to do when you can't find a cache', below).
- 'Write a note' – notes are not logged as 'finds', but are used when you have something to say, for example that the cache logbook is full and needs replacing, or that you passed by the cache (having previously discovered it) and want to record that everything is okay with it.
- 'Needs archiving' – choose this option if you found a serious problem with the cache, for example, if it is badly damaged. An archived cache is not active, but remains in the database so that its information page can be viewed to discover why it was archived.
- 'Needs maintenance' – means just that; the cache is damaged, wet, irreparable, etc, and needs the attention of the owner.

If you have a number of caches to log entries for, then there is a little trick to speed up the process. It starts when you identify the caches you are going in search of. Go to the Navigation panel on the cache page, and select 'Watch listing'. This will add the cache(s) to a page known as your 'Watchlist', which is accessible from your profile page. When you return home, simply go to your Watchlist and select the caches you have found; it's much quicker this way, even though this may not have been the original intention of the Watchlist. You should do this with all the caches you are going out to find; it just makes keeping a record a little easier. Once you have logged your find, remember to remove the cache from your Watchlist.

DISCOVERING A GEOCACHE

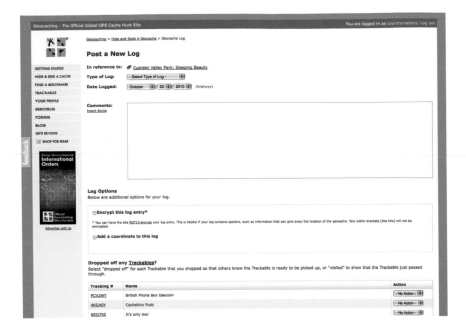

Geocaching > Hide and Seek A Geocache > Geocache Log

Post a New Log

GETTING STARTED
HIDE & SEEK A CACHE
FIND A BENCHMARK
TRACKABLES
YOUR PROFILE
RESOURCES
FORUMS
BLOG
GPS REVIEWS
SHOP FOR GEAR

Shop Groundspeak
International Orders

Official Geocaching Merchandise
Advertise with Us

In reference to: Cuerden Valley Park: Sleeping Beauty
Type of Log: - Select Type of Log -
Date Logged: October 22 2010 (M/d/yyyy)

Comments:
Insert Smile

Log Options
Below are additional options for your log.

☐ Encrypt this log entry*

* You can have the site ROT13 encrypt your log entry. This is helpful if your log contains spoilers, such as information that can give away the location of the geocache. Text within brackets [like this] will not be encrypted.

☐ Add a coordinate to this log

Dropped off any Trackables?
Select "dropped off" for each Trackable that you dropped so that others know the Trackable is ready to be picked up, or "visited" to show that the Trackable just passed through.

Tracking #	Name	Action
PCV2WY	British Phone Box Geocoin	- No Action -
4KG4OY	Cachekinz Pudz	- No Action -
KEQ7SQ	It's only me!	- No Action -

'Post a new log' page

- 'Attended' – is the entry you make if you attend an event cache: this 'Type of log' option appears on the screen only for event caches.
- 'Webcam photo taken' – is the correct log type for webcam caches, which although 'discontinued' still have a number of active locations around the country. This log-type option appears only for webcam caches.

The second field on the 'Post a new log' page is the **date**, which defaults to the current date, but if this does not correspond with the date on which you actually made the find, then simply change it.

The third field is where you enter any **comments** you want to make about your experience, whether you enjoyed it, had terrain difficulties, fell in a river, met other geocachers, had to avoid muggles, cows, bulls… whatever you want to say. But it is important to say something – part of the fun of placing caches is the pleasure derived from others finding them and saying something nice about your efforts. So you should do the same in return.

Sometimes, in your comment, you may want to make reference to something that will give a clue to the cache location. To avoid this appearing too readily to those who have not yet found the cache, you have the option to encrypt the whole or part of your comment by selecting the 'Encrypt this log entry' key below the Comments panel. For example, comments like 'We had to use a long stick to unhook the cache from the tree branch' is something of a give-away that you might want to encrypt. If you do decide to encrypt a comment, then note that text within square brackets – [What a great cache!] – will not be encrypted. So you can put all your 'open' comments in square brackets, leaving sections of your comments without brackets so that they become encrypted. There are no hard and fast rules about this; it is your decision.

When you have completed your log, simply click on 'Submit log entry'.

UPLOADING PICTURES

You might also want to upload a picture or two taken at the cache location, but be careful not to give too much away – be wary of conspicuous features in the background, for example. Geocaching is family fun, and it is great for children to have their pictures on the website showing them holding the cache container.

Uploading pictures from your computer is not difficult. Once you have logged your find, you go to a 'View Geocache Log' page. Click on 'Upoad image' in the top right hand corner to go through to 'Uploading for Log'. Choose the image from those on your computer, write a caption and click on 'Upload'.

The system supports the normal picture formats – jpg, gif and tif – although all the final images are converted to jpg format.

A micro cache concealed in the hollowed-out base of a small log

6

DISCOVERING A GEOCACHE

Gordale Scar in the Yorkshire Dales National Park poses a problem for walkers wanting to go up, but for geocachers is an easy EarthCache

ADDING A WAYPOINT

There are times when you find a cache and discover that the co-ordinates on your GPS receiver do not correspond with those on the cache page. Slight differences are tolerable and to be expected, but if there is a significant difference, **and you can be certain that you were receiving a strong satellite signal**, then you can post your co-ordinates on the website by ticking the box marked 'Add a waypoint to the log' on the 'Post a new log' page. Of course, you should then post a 'Comment' to explain why you found the co-ordinates to be different.

WHAT TO DO WHEN YOU CAN'T FIND A CACHE

There are only two reasons why caches are not found – the first is that they are no longer there (muggled or moved by animals), and the second is the level of your diligence. The latter is something that improves the more you geocache. The greater your experience, the more readily you can spot likely cache locations that you might previously have overlooked. It's no shame not to find a cache; finding them takes practice. Do not be put off. Speak to any experienced geocacher and they will tell you many stories of caches they were unable to find, even of taking three or four attempts to find a cache that everyone else seemed to find easy to locate.

But the components of diligence in this context are many.

- How much time were you able to devote to your search?
- Are you sure that you had the correct co-ordinates?
- Was there adequate satellite coverage to give you a strong signal?
- Did you check the log entries to see if others had also failed to find the cache?
- Did you check the hint?
- Were there too many muggles about?
- Was it getting dark?
- Were you systematic in your search?
- Were you distracted at a critical moment?

Whether it was because the cache was lost or you simply couldn't spot it, it is good practice to log 'Didn't find it' – what in geo-speak is called a 'DNF'. This alerts the owner to the possibility that the cache may have gone missing and may need replacing. The owner is not going to respond to just a single DNF, but if a series appears then it is a safe bet that something is awry.

It is equally important to return to a cache you couldn't find first time round in order to search again. Geocaching is a fun activity; don't take it too seriously. When you do find the cache, you'll be wondering how you missed it the first time. It happens to everyone!

If you do fail to find, add the cache to your Watchlist. If anyone else finds, or does not find, the cache, you will receive a note to that effect. If there is a string of DNFs, then you can feel moderately satisfied; it wasn't your fault. But if others come along and find the cache with ease, then you know what to do. Do not log a DNF if you didn't really look for the cache – perhaps because it was raining or there were too many muggles about. Log a DNF only if you genuinely searched (for more than a few seconds), but didn't find the cache. DNRB (Did not really bother) and DNT (Did not try) don't count.

6

DISCOVERING A GEOCACHE

The stunning landscape around Elgol on the Isle of Skye makes this a perfect candidate for an EarthCache

7 CREATING GEOCACHES

Sooner or later you will want to try creating caches yourself, and this is every bit as enjoyable and challenging as searching for them. But it is something that requires a little forethought if you are to earn a reputation for quality caches. It is like writing a book – you begin with an idea, spend time planning and giving the idea shape, then give form to the idea, and finally sit back and see what people have to say about your handiwork.

Adding your own caches to the ever increasing number throughout the world involves

- deciding on the type of geocache to create
- selecting a container
- selecting a good hiding place
- determining the co-ordinates
- deciding on the cache contents
- submitting the cache for review (ie getting your cache published)
- maintaining the geocache.

Full guidelines on creating geocaches are contained on www.geocaching.com – begin by looking in 'Hide and seek a cache'. They are quite extensive and give a lot of detail, and the key points are summarised in the following paragraphs. When creating a cache you are required to indicate that you have read and understood these guidelines. Because all caches are located on someone's land, a team of reviewers will look at the details of your proposed cache to check whether it can be published on the website (see 'Submitting a geocache for review', below).

DECIDING ON THE TYPE OF GEOCACHE TO CREATE

The easiest type of cache to begin with is a **traditional cache**, the basic format. As a minimum your traditional cache must contain a logbook in some form.

One of the reasons for choosing a simple, straightforward cache type to begin with is that placing caches comes with an obligation to maintain them – in other words, checking them periodically, responding to logs telling you that the logbook is full/wet/missing, and so on. By keeping things simple to start with, you learn just how much is involved

It makes sense not to attempt to place caches yourself until you have spent some time discovering how other geocachers do it. Searching for caches teaches you what to take into consideration when deciding on your own cache locations, and gives you ideas for hiding your own.

in placing caches. If you are happy with the responsibility, then go ahead and place more. But, and this is a plea on behalf of all geocachers, if you feel you might be unable to maintain a cache, please do not place it.

Whether you move on to creating **multi-caches** or **puzzle caches** is something you can decide once you have a clear understanding of the sort of skills that are involved in creating these caches. It is hugely rewarding to create a puzzle cache, for example, but you have to be certain that the solution to the puzzle really does give the correct information, and only the correct information. For example, the binary code:

01001110 00100000 00110101 00110011 11000010 10110000 00100000 00110100
00110010 00101110 00110110 00110110 00110000 00001101 00001010 01010111
00100000 00110000 00110000 00110010 11000010 10110000 00100000 00110011
00111000 00101110 00111001 00110001 00110100 00001101 00001010

translates as:

N 53° 42.660
W 002° 38.914

Even the slightest error while inputting this sort of eye-boggling information can result in wide deviations. So, to be certain that you have your encoding done correctly, you need a code translator, and there are a number of these on the internet. It is advisable to encode and decode the information a couple of times to be sure you have it correct (see 'Geocaching co-ordinates checker' in Chapter 10).

SELECTING A CONTAINER

The simplest form of container to use is the plastic food container with four lock-down clips, available from most supermarkets. The container should be waterproof, for obvious reasons, as you will discover when you find some that were not.

A magnetic nano

A Pelican container

There may be many other suitable containers about your house, but for ease of getting started spend a little to buy some of the Tupperware-like boxes and a supply of small notebooks to serve as logbooks. You might want to be indulgent and buy pencils and pencil sharpeners to place in the container, but if you don't you need to alert other geocachers to the fact that they will have to bring a pen to sign the log. You do that in the cache description.

The beauty of the food-container type of box is that it allows for the placement of trade items and trackable items (see Chapter 8). This makes the cache more attractive to seekers. This type of container will serve equally well for the type of caches that are a little more challenging, such as multi-caches, puzzle caches and letterbox hybrids.

Other domestic containers that you can use include plastic medicine bottles, 35mm film canisters, and anything else that can be locked. Large boxes are generally easy to find, but at the other extreme there are cache containers known as nanos, and these are very small, no more than a centimetre in diameter. They are also magnetic and can simply be fixed to any metal surface, thus blending in well with the background.

There is no particular need to invest in purpose-made cache containers, but they do have printed on them a notice that they are an 'Official geocache' and part of a worldwide game. It enhances the image of the game if containers are properly labelled.

To make the pursuit even more interesting, it is possible to buy cache containers that are disguised as rocks, bolts, capsules, acorns, mushrooms, pine cones and a whole imaginative range of items. The aim is to make geocaching as challenging as possible, to encourage observation and search skills... and to develop persistence!

SELECTING A GOOD LOCATION AND HIDING PLACE

By now you will have found a few caches yourself, and will be getting an idea of the sort of locations that are suitable for hiding a cache. On your travels you may well have already noticed a few likely places.

If you create a cache more than 50 miles from your home, it is unlikely that the details will be published on the website. You have a maintenance responsibility – so keep things local unless you can guarantee that some else will maintain your distant cache.

The first golden rule is that you must think carefully about how your cache and the actions of fellow geocachers might be perceived by the public. A cache concealed in

To prolong the life of your caches use only containers that are watertight. Film canisters are fine in dry summer conditions, but they are not watertight. Ideal as they may be in terms of size, they do deteriorate very quickly. If you do use a film canister, then wrap the log sheet in a plastic wallet to help keep it dry.

Use black or camouflage tape or paint to cover the plastic container and make it more difficult to detect. You can also buy camouflage bags in which to conceal containers.

7

CREATING GEOCACHES

Disguised cache containers: pine cone, bolt, mushroom

In public areas, avoid using containers that may appear suspicious, and do not secure them with wires or tape. To reduce confusion and alarm when a cache is discovered accidentally, clearly label your container on the outside with appropriate information to say it is a geocache and harmless. You can buy pre-printed labels to stick on the cache indicating that it is an official geocache and part of a game, so use these if you can or improvise appropriately.

full view of offices or apartments, for example, risks having geocachers regarded as suspicious.

If in doubt, find another location – the UK has only about 60,000 caches, so there is plenty of room. There are many popular locations such as the base/roots of trees, among logs, under rocks, in crevices, under bridges (provided this can be accomplished safely), in bird feeders hanging from trees, and in a host of places if you are using magnetic containers. Much thought needs to go into choosing the right place; don't just select somewhere at random because it conveniently has a nice hidey hole.

A concealed cache should not be easily visible to a passer-by. Use creativity and imagination to find a challenging place.

CACHE SATURATION

You should not place caches in an area already well covered by caches. It is a requirement of www.geocaching.com that physical caches are separated by at least 0.1 miles (161m/528ft) in a direct line – although caches that lie on either side of a river, where the walk to each is greater than the prescribed distance, would be acceptable.

The aim of this requirement is to encourage the placing of caches in areas not already covered. Do not place caches every 600ft, just because you can. Be a little more imaginative and earn yourself a reputation as a considerate geocache owner.

Pre-printed labels for affixing to cache containers

PERMANENCE AND PERMISSION

You must remember that your cache needs a significant degree of permanence about it, so do not place caches that might disintegrate, be swept away by flood water, fall from the hiding place, and so on.

You also need to ensure that you have the permission of the owner of the land on which the cache is placed before you hide the cache. Some organisations (listed on www.gagb. co.uk), including the National Trust, the Woodland Trust and the Forestry Commission, give guidelines on their respective websites, but you will be asked to confirm when submitting your cache for review either that you have been given permission to place your cache, or that the landowner has given a blanket consent to geocaching. In some instances you will need to apply to the landowner for consent to place a cache on their land. Several landowners, such as the Woodland Trust, have downloadable forms on their website for this purpose.

Bear in mind that geocaching is still a new activity, and many people do not understand what it is; take the time to explain.

WHERE NOT TO HIDE A CACHE

There are quite a few places where you should not conceal caches, and for your cache to be listed on www.geocaching. com it needs to meet certain criteria. Generally, caches should not be

- **buried** – it is fine to cover a cache with branches, leaves, stones and rocks, but it is not acceptable to hide a cache by digging
- **within environmentally sensitive areas**, including nature reserves, sites of special scientific interest, sites of biodiversity importance, archaeological sites, or any place where human activity might disturb wildlife

Caches that take players to historical locations are always popular (this is Castle Bolton in North Yorkshire), but if you are placing a cache in such places, do be sure to get the landowner's permission first

- **close to railway lines**, unless there is some adequate fencing to prevent access to the lines
- anywhere that might **cause concern for public safety or about terrorist activity**, such as near airports, tunnels, bridges, military installations, local water supplies or government buildings.

DETERMINING THE CO-ORDINATES

Once you have found the perfect place for a cache, you need to determine its co-ordinates, and to do so as precisely as you can. First, remember to ensure that your GPS device is using the WGS84 datum, and that it is set to use degrees and decimal minutes – hddd*mm.mmm.

Getting accurate co-ordinates is probably the most difficult thing about placing a cache. There are many factors that can produce variations, and you may find that the co-ordinates change from minute to minute. If you are out in the open, the chances are that you will get good satellite coverage and can therefore produce very good co-ordinates. But if your cache is in woodland, for example, it may not be so easy to get a clear reading. And there are certain times of day when satellite coverage is greater than at others; this will affect the accuracy, too.

To begin with, have your GPS device turned on as you approach the cache location. Then, as you reach the hiding place, note the co-ordinates. Now walk on by and turn round to come back, making another note of the co-ordinates. Do this a few times, and you can see which co-ordinates are the most likely to be accurate. (Note that some GPS devices have an averaging feature that compares co-ordinates at a single spot over a few minutes, and then averages the result.) If you are with someone else who has a GPS, get them to check the reading, too.

Finally, once back home, you can check the co-ordinates on Google Earth. This is not always wholly reliable, and should not be used for calculating co-ordinates. But the clarity of Google Earth is often such that you can actually see the mound of rocks beneath which you placed the cache, and can compare the readings. If you get widely differing results, you may have to check the co-ordinates out in the field once more. But if in doubt use the figures on your GPS device.

CACHE CONTENTS

Use common sense when choosing the contents. Explosives, fireworks, knives, drugs, alcohol and other illicit items should not be placed in a cache. Geocaching is a family activity and cache contents should be suitable for all ages.

Food items are always a bad idea, and in some cases caches have been chewed through and destroyed by animals because food items (or items that smell like food) are in the cache.

If the original cache contents lists questionable items, or if a cache is subsequently reported to contain questionable items, the cache may be disabled by the reviewers, and the owner of the cache contacted and asked to remove the items before the cache is enabled.

CACHES THAT SOLICIT AND COMMERCIAL CACHES

Caches posted for religious, political, charitable or social reasons, or which solicit support for such causes, are not permitted. Geocaching is supposed to be a light, fun activity, and not to have a hidden agenda.

Commercial caches will not be published on www.geocaching.com without prior approval. A commercial cache is a geocache listing, or actual geocache, which is perceived to have been submitted with the principal or substantial intent of soliciting customers or generating commercial gain. The geocache is presumed to be commercial if the finder is required to go inside a business, interact with employees, and/or purchase a product or service, or if the cache listing has overtones of advertising, marketing or promotion.

SUBMITTING A GEOCACHE FOR REVIEW

Geocaching is a self-regulating activity, but one that adheres to a number of guidelines. To ensure that you have followed those guidelines, a team of 'reviewers' will look at the details of your proposed cache before it can be published on www.geocaching.com. In order to submit a cache you will have to indicate that you have read and understood the extensive guidelines on listing requirements. During the review process, a reviewer checks the page for inaccuracies, poor co-ordinates and compliance with the guidelines. If the reviewer has any reservations about your cache, he/she will temporarily archive the cache pending clarification.

One of the principal reasons for a cache not being published is its proximity to other caches (see 'Cache saturation', above). It is easy to check the whereabouts of traditional caches, because their location is on the website. But, unless you tackle all the multi-caches in the area, you won't know the location of any final or bonus caches, and they may be close to your intended place.

It is a requirement that your cache should already be in place before you submit it for review. From one point of view, this is odd, because if it is not published, then you have to go out again and retrieve the cache. From another point of view, requiring the cache to be in place is sensible because it becomes live the moment the reviewer publishes it, and therefore needs to be in place. Some geocachers like to specialise in being the 'First to Find' new caches, so your cache has to be there for them to find from the outset.

THE REVIEW PROCESS

Begin the review process by selecting 'Hide and seek a cache' from the home page of the website. This takes you to a two-part page, with 'Hide a cache' on the right. Within this panel is a link to an Online Form, and you should select this to be redirected to a page headed 'Report a new cache'. This is what you are now going to do.

There are a number of fields on this page.

- **Cache type**: select the relevant type, such as 'traditional cache'.
- **Cache size**: select one of the options from the drop-down menu.
- **Cache name**: this is where you give the cache a name. Think of something imaginative and relevant to the location. If you are entering more than one cache as part of a series, begin with the series name, such as 'White Cliffs of Dover: Lighthouse'.
- **Who placed the cache**: this is where you enter your geocaching pseudonym.

- **Date placed**: this will default to the current date, but can be adjusted if you don't want the cache to go live until a later date.
- **Related web page**: if you have created a separate web page relating to the cache, this is the place to enter the URL (website address).
- **Background image URL**: enables you to change the background image on the web page to a location of your choosing.
- **Co-ordinates**: this is where you enter the cache co-ordinates.
- **Location**: defaults to 'United Kingdom', but can be changed; it also defaults to the region of Britain that your home co-ordinates slot into.

- **Overall difficulty rating**: this is where you grade the difficulty of your cache in increments of half a point. For this, and the terrain rating below, there is a sub-system that allows you to enter information about your cache, and which will then generate a suggested rating for it. You don't have to accept it, but entries that give inaccurate ratings are misleading, so you may want to be guided by the system.
- **Overall terrain rating**: the terrain rating indicates how easy it is to get to the cache location. Anything rated 2 or less is generally accepted as being accessible by wheelchairs and buggies. The highest grade (5) should be reserved for the most difficult terrain or ascents of mountains: the cache on the summit of Ben More on the Isle of Mull (GCTFPZ) is rated 5 for terrain – it's a long climb from sea level – although the difficulty rating is only 2.5. If you are uncertain, use the in-built system to see what rating the website suggests, and use this as a guide.
- **Cache details**: In entering the cache details, you can use html coding (with the exception of JavaScript and other embedded code), if you know how to, in any of the description fields that follow. If you do supply html, you will need to tick a box below for the text to render correctly.
- **Short description**: is just that, and is intended to give location information, along with notes on the terrain and general difficulty levels; this is limited to 500 characters.
- **Long description**: there is no character limit on this field, and here you should impart information about the cache. This is where you 'sell' the cache to other geocachers – include historical, wildlife, landscape, architectural and other notes, in fact anything that makes the

cache interesting. You can enter the information using html coding, but this is not essential; the key point is to tell geocachers what your cache is about, and why it is placed where it is.

- **Hints**: Any hints about the location of the cache will be encrypted. How much information you give, and how cryptic the message, is up to you. You can be fairly explicit – 'Under stile beside fence' – or a little obtuse – 'Lowly, bolely, holey'. Giving hints is a skill in itself. Wait until you have tried finding caches without using a hint, and you will understand. You will also see what level of clue you need to give. Something a little bit out of the ordinary is quite acceptable – it makes searchers think. But, at the end of the day, you want your cache to be found, so think carefully about your hints.

- **Note to reviewer**: in order to speed up the publishing process, you need to provide details of your cache that will help the reviewer. The reviewer deletes the note before your cache is published, although if you access your listing in the meantime – perhaps to edit it – then the note to reviewer will appear. In this section you need to explain that you have permission to place the cache where it is, or otherwise give information that will help the reviewer to publish it quickly. If the reviewer has any concerns about your cache, he/she will contact you and explain what those concerns are to give you a chance to amend the listing or provide

Canal towpaths and adjacent land make excellent locations for cache concealment

further information. This is the normal procedure and applies to everyone.

Finally, you will be required to tick the boxes at the bottom of the page to confirm that you have read and understood the guidelines for listing a cache, and that you agree to the terms of use agreement. Then simply click on 'Report new listing' and wait.

In the meantime, you can continue to edit your listing, if you realise that you've made a mistake or want to clarify something. There is an immediate option to edit your listing as soon as you submit it – the page is self-explanatory. But if you have second thoughts a little later, then select 'My profile' from the home page of the website, and on the 'Your profile' page select '(Yours)', next to 'Geocaches' near the top of the page. Your pending cache will be listed there, and you can access it and make changes by using the 'Edit listing' option in the Navigation panel.

MAINTAINING A GEOCACHE

The process of placing a geocache carries with it the responsibility of maintaining the cache, which is a good reason for not placing caches too far from your home. In fact, if the reviewer notices that your cache is a long way from your home co-ordinates, and you have not made any arrangement with a local geocacher to maintain it, the cache may well not be approved.

You should plan on visiting your cache from time to time to check on its condition, but, more importantly, do so as soon as possible after receiving an online log entry indicating that the cache needs maintenance. Often it may involve nothing more than replacing a full logbook, but caches do become waterlogged, either through direct water penetration or by condensation, and it is your responsibility to 'repair' whatever is the damage. Occasionally, you may need to replace the entire cache container with a new one.

When you visit your cache, check that the area around it is not becoming trampled by geocachers searching for it and creating paths leading to the cache. If necessary, consider relocating your cache or permanently removing it. If you take either of these actions, remember to post a note on the cache page on the website. If you do permanently remove a cache, then also remember to archive it in the database – that makes your cache inactive so that people don't go searching for something that is no longer there.

Whenever someone finds, or doesn't find, your cache, you receive an email to that effect. Be sure to read the log entries – they can alert you to the need to carry out maintenance.

There is nothing worse than finding a cache that is not maintained, but left to deteriorate – there is no fun in that!

7

CREATING GEOCACHES

PUTTING A CACHE UP FOR ADOPTION

Occasionally you may not be able to maintain your own caches – perhaps you are moving away from the area, for example. Because it is essential that caches are always properly maintained, if you find yourself in this position, then try to put your caches up for adoption by someone local.

How you do this depends on how well you know your local geocaching community. It is unlikely that you will find no one willing to take over your caches, and all you need to do is get their consent to do so. If all else fails, then try writing a note into the relevant cache pages saying that you are looking for someone to adopt your cache(s).

Once you have someone willing to take over your caches, then go to www.geocaching.com/adopt and enter the code of the cache you are putting up for adoption. This will take you through to a page on which you enter the user name of the person who is adopting your cache. When finished, click on 'Send adoption request', and the system does the rest.

If the process is being done in reverse – you are adopting someone else's caches – then when you receive notification that the cache has been transferred to you, it is courtesy to acknowledge the transfer somewhere on the cache page, in one of the description panels (see GCXMFA).

MAINTENANCE GUIDELINES

The geocaching guidelines specify that 'As the cache owner, you are responsible for physically checking your cache periodically, and especially when someone reports a problem with the cache (missing, damaged, wet, etc). You may temporarily disable your cache to let others know not to hunt for it until you have a chance to fix the problem. This feature is to allow you a reasonable time – normally a few weeks – in which to arrange a visit to your cache. In the event that a cache is not being properly maintained, or has been temporarily disabled for an extended period of time, the listing may be archived.'

CACHES THAT HAVE NOT BEEN MAINTAINED

During your geocaching expeditions, you may encounter caches that have not been maintained. This could be for a variety of reasons. The first step in the procedure for getting the cache serviced is to post a 'Needs maintenance' note on the website. This alerts the owner to the fact that something needs to be done about the cache.

However, the owner may no longer be involved in geo-caching, which effectively leaves the cache high and dry, or (more to the point) low and very wet. There is no provision for you to simply take over ownership of the cache; it belongs to someone else (although if some kind fairy were to visit the cache and replace the container with a new one, who would know?).

But you can contact the owner and offer to take over the ownership. There is a procedure that allows this, and contacting the owner is the first step. But if the owner does not respond, all you can do is contact one of the reviewers and ask for the cache to be archived. The reviewer will follow a procedure that ultimately leads to the cache being archived. This then allows you to go out and create a new cache at that location.

DELETING LOG ENTRIES

Very occasionally, log entries may be inappropriate. If this is the case, then as cache owner you can delete them – go to 'Your profile', then select '(Yours)', next to 'Geocaches'. Select the cache in question and scroll down to the log entries. Find the offending log and select 'View this log'. You will then find a page 'View a cache log', on which you can select 'Delete log'. Of course, this should be used only as a last resort, and it may be worth contacting the person who wrote the log and asking them to change it.

CREATING AN EARTHCACHE

Because EarthCaches do not have a physical cache container, and are intended to serve a different purpose from conventional caches, there is a different set of guidelines for those wanting to create an EarthCache. All EarthCache sites are subject to the normal review process. The guidelines are viewable in detail on www.geosociety.org/earthcache/guidelines.htm, but are summarised here

- EarthCache sites must provide Earth science lessons
- EarthCache sites must be educational
- EarthCache sites can be a single site or a multiple virtual cache
- EarthCaches should highlight a unique feature
- EarthCache sites follow the geocaching principles and adhere to the principles of 'Leave No Trace' outdoor ethics
- logging of an EarthCache must involve visitors undertaking some educational task that relates to the Earth science at the site
- all EarthCache sites developed must have prior approval of the landowners before submission (depending on local country laws and customs)
- damage to the site is unacceptable.

This obelisk, in the Snowdonia National Park in North Wales, is the sort of thing to expect of a cache with a 5/5 rating

8 TRACKABLE ITEMS

As you discover more and more caches you will inevitably encounter what are known as trackable items. These take two forms – 'travel bugs' and 'geocoins'. Images of geocoins are dotted throughout these pages.

The purpose of trackable items (also known as 'hitch-hikers') is for them to be transported from cache to cache, usually in accordance with some basic idea – such as 'to visit mountain caches', 'to travel the world', 'to visit every country', 'to travel around national parks', and so on. It is for the owners of trackable items to assign a purpose. In reality, most owners keep it simple – 'to travel to as many caches as possible' – but there are some more difficult requirements to comply with – 'to visit caches at surfing beaches', 'to visit caches that begin with the letter R' (for example), 'to visit caches beginning with successive letters of the alphabet'. When a trackable item is picked up from a cache, the finder logs it on the website and, later, records where it is dropped off, so that 'owners' can track these items on their journey.

A geocoin (one example of the many colourful designs scattered throughout this book)

> Finding and moving on trackable items is an exciting and fascinating part of geocaching, especially when you find one that has travelled the world many times over. Geocoins in particular are of outstanding design, and have become collectable items; not that you should keep any you find in caches. That is not in the spirit of geocaching.

TRAVEL BUGS

A travel bug, usually abbreviated to TB, takes the basic form of a two-part dog tag with a unique reference number. Usually owners of TBs will attach something (anything reasonable) to the tag, such as a golf ball, key ring, toy car, doll or even junk cleared out from caches.

Picking up a travel bug

There is no obligation to remove a TB from a cache, you can simply note its number and then 'Discover' it on the TB's home page. But most people do take them, with the

Travel bug tags (this is a dummy – tracking numbers should never be disclosed)

intention of moving them on. If you do pick up a TB, record this on the website as follows.

- Locate the unique tracking number, which is stamped on the dog tag. If you are intending to move the trackable on immediately (before returning home from your geocaching trip), then make a note of this number so that you can record what you've done online later.
- Once back at your computer, select 'Trackable items' from the left-hand menu and enter the unique number in the 'Enter tracking number' field. Then select 'Track' to go through to the TB's own page.
- At the TB's page, select 'Add a log entry' from the Trackable Items Options panel.
- Now 'Post a new log' in the same way you would for finding a cache, but inserting the unique number in the 'Travel bug tracking' field, and write some comments so that the owner knows where the trackable is, and what's happening to it.
- Once you have completed this process you will find that the name of the trackable has been added to an inventory at the bottom of the right-hand panel on 'Your profile' page. This is 'Your inventory', and it contains a list of trackable items currently in your possession.

Bear in mind that trackable items are meant to be moved on, and you should endeavour to do so within a period of two weeks. If it is likely to take longer than this, then you should contact the owner by email, as a matter of courtesy, and let them know when you hope to move on the item.

From time to time you will find that the TBs listed in the inventory on the cache page are not present in the cache container. There are a number of possible reasons for this.

- Someone got to it ahead of you and has yet to record that it has been retrieved – this often happens when someone is on holiday without access to the internet.
- It was never there in the first place; the previous 'finder' entered the information on the wrong cache page.
- It has been stolen, usually by a muggle, but sometimes, if it was a particularly attractive TB, by a geocacher not playing the game; activated travel bugs do occasionally turn up on online auction sites.

Dropping off a travel bug

Once you have logged that you have retrieved a TB, you can now physically drop it off into another cache. When you log your visit to the cache in which you have placed the TB, then as part of that process go to the bottom of the page for logging finds and locate the TB you left. Click on the box at the right of this panel and select 'Dropped off'.

A well-travelled travel bug, with post-box attachment

Then select 'Submit your log entry'. If you forget to log the TB drop you can always edit your log entry or 'Write a note' saying something like 'TB drop'.

If the TB has a purpose or goal, try to comply with it as closely as possible – if the goal is to take the TB to the seaside, don't leave it on a mountain, for example; if it wants to go north, don't take it south. If you realise that you can't comply with the TB's mission, then either put it back where you found it or place it in a cache that might help it on its way – for example, a TB that wants to visit Australia could be dropped in a cache near an airport.

To record where you dropped off a TB

- visit the cache page, as you would to record your find – if you have already logged your find, don't worry, simply 'Write a note' instead, and drop the TB into the page
- complete the various fields for logging a find (or writing a note)
- select the name of the TB you have dropped off from the inventory at the bottom of the page (if you dropped off more than one, then do the same with all the bugs you dropped off)
- submit your log – the TBs will transfer from your inventory to the online cache page.

Your own travel bugs
When you buy a new dog-tag TB – they are available online at many outlets – it comes in two parts. One is the travelling tag and the other is the owner's, marked as a 'Copy'. Both are the owner's property. It is unusual for unattached dog tags alone to be left in caches – more commonplace is for the owner to attach an object that can be used to give the TB a sense of purpose. These range from small key rings to golf balls, teddy bears, toy dogs, toy cars – anything, in fact, that lends a little interest to the items.

Each dog tag is stamped with a unique tracking number, by which the item is identified. But before you can do anything with it, the tag must be activated – a simple process.

Activating a travel bug
- Select 'Trackable items' from the left-hand menu on the www.geocaching.com home page.
- On the 'Trackable items' page enter the unique reference number in the field marked 'Activate trackable items', and select 'Activate'.
- You will next be asked to enter an activation code; this appears on or in the packet containing the travel bug. Enter the activation code and select 'Activate your trackable item'.

TRACKABLE ITEMS

Black Rock Cottage along the West Highland Way is the location of a popular traditional cache

- The website automatically generates a TB reference number, which is not the same as the tracking number on the actual TB. The reference number (also known as the TB number) can be confused with the number on the dog tag. The TB number is the code on each TB's page, which is the 'safe' number to help users reference each TB without giving out the bug's actual tracking number.

- You can give the travel bug a name, or just leave it at 'Travel bug dog tag', then assign a mission to it. What do you want it to do? It could visit mountains, railway stations, parks, waterfalls... and so on. It makes sense to prescribe a mission that is easily achieved, and which therefore generates a history worth following, rather than a mission to visit South Africa or Australia. These missions are possible, but unless your TB is discovered by someone who is going there, it is unlikely to follow its mission. And once the TB reaches South Africa or Australia, its mission is complete and the TB technically redundant.
- Finally, enter a brief description of the tag and anything you may attach to it. Select 'Edit trackable item's description', and on the next page complete the fields marked 'Location activated', and select 'Complete activation'.
- Activation is now complete, and your trackable item has its own home page.

Keeping tabs on your TB
Once you have placed your TB in a cache, sit back and wait to see if anyone finds it and moves it on. When someone does log a find, you will receive an email telling you so.

On 'Your profile' page, select '(Yours)', next to 'Trackable items', and this takes you to a 'Search trackable items' page, where all your own trackable items are listed. You can see at a glance where your trackable is currently located, and, in the right-hand column, how far it has travelled since you originally placed it.

Click on one of the trackable names, and you are taken to the individual page for that item – one that shows the history of your item, who found it, who moved it, and to where. The line 'Tracking history' gives the distance the item has travelled. Select 'View map', and the item's journeys are illustrated on a world map.

GEOCOINS
A geocoin is a special coin created by individuals or groups of geocachers as a 'signature item' or 'calling card'; many of them are associated with geocaching events. Like TBs,

TRACKABLE ITEMS

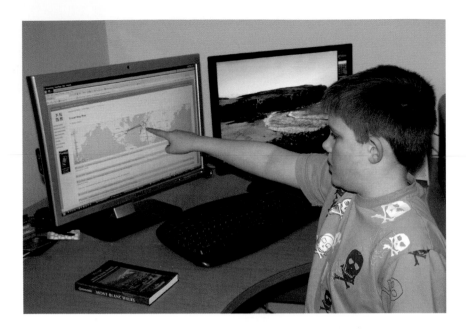

Following the journeys of a trackable item are a good way of generating a world geography lesson for young children (and adults, too)

each geocoin is assigned a unique tracking number, which allows them to travel from cache to cache or to be passed among friends, picking up stories along the way.

Picking up and dropping off geocoins

The procedure for picking up geocoins from caches, and for ensuring their onward travel, is exactly the same as for TBs.

Discovery

One of the options you have on finding either a TB or a geocoin is to leave it where it is and simply 'Discover' it. This means that you are recording the fact that you found it, but didn't take it. You will find that on the 'Found it. Log it' page, this posting option becomes available to you.

Geocoins near you

If you select 'Trackable items' from the website home page, and then select 'Geocoin home', you will be taken to a page with a Google Map that shows the location of all geocoins close to your home co-ordinates. You can click on the coin image on the map to view its details.

Collecting geocoins

The design of most geocoins is quite stunning, and not surprisingly they have become collectors' items. But, since geocoins, once activated, are the trackable property of the owner, they are not yours for the keeping. You must 'play

Typical geocoins

the game' and move them on. If you want to collect geo-coins, there are many available for purchase on the internet.

Tracking your geocoins
You can track your geocoins in exactly the same way that you track a TB (see above).

'MOBILE' TRACKABLE ITEMS
To extend the 'discovery' element of trackable items, it is possible to acquire magnetic or adhesive TBs that you can affix to items such as your car, so turning it into a mobile TB – although you should make it clear on the TB's page that it is not for moving on (see TB33TDH). Alternatively, you could fasten TBs to your keyring or wear them as jewellery. When you find a mobile TB, simply make a note of its code and then log your 'discovery' of it. The author often wears a trackable T-shirt to event caches; it has a valid tracking number and so can be 'discovered'.

8

TRACKABLE ITEMS

A stunning dolerite sill intrusion EarthCache at Rubn an'Dunain, Isle of Skye

9 GROUNDSPEAK AND WWW.GEOCACHING.COM

GEOCACHING.COM

Groundspeak is the parent company for geocaching; it is a privately held company based in Seattle, Washington. The company evolved almost immediately after the US government turned off selective availability on its GPS satellites in May 2000, and the first cache was placed within 24 hours. Within three days, two others had used their GPS devices to locate the cache; during the next week more did the same, and geocaching was born.

The building of the geocaching.com website was to come within four months, dedicated to the role location-based technology could play in outdoor recreation. When the website was launched in September 2000, there were just 75 caches worldwide. At the time of writing (October 2010), there are 1,214,914.

BENEFITS OF PREMIUM MEMBERSHIP

To use the website you have to become a member, and there are two levels of membership available. The **basic level** of membership, which is free, allows only two functions

- to view co-ordinates and location information for geocaches
- to write about your finds and your experiences on the website.

In addition, **premium membership**, which costs $30 a year (2010), gives access to website features and functionality that will enhance your geocaching experience. These include

- organising your favourites – you can create 'favourites' lists, such as dog friendly, puzzle caches, etc, using a Bookmark feature (see 'Manage bookmarks', below)
- creating custom searches – downloading up to 1000 waypoints, based on cache size, location, attributes, etc – using Pocket Queries (see below)
- searching for geocaches along a particular route
- accessing other related websites, including www.waymarking.com and www.whereigo.com
- receiving Instant Notifications of new caches to enable you to be the First To Find (FTF).

GROUNDSPEAK NEWSLETTER

Groundspeak issue a weekly newsletter containing information about forthcoming Mega-events, news items and

9

general events. There is a strong US element, but the section on 'Upcoming events' is especially useful to geocachers in the UK.

Also listed are recent additions to the cache database. These are based on your home co-ordinates and therefore feature caches close to where you live.

YOUR ACCOUNT DETAILS

The page listing your account details is where you provide basic information about yourself. Some of the information is, by default, not public; other information is limited by yourself to just that degree of information you wish to disclose.

You can access your account details most easily by selecting 'My profile' or 'Your profile' from the website home page. Then selection 'Your account details' from the top menu. This includes key information about your account with Groundspeak, allows you to upload a photograph of yourself, and gives details of your membership and the date of renewal, along with the email address associated with www.geocaching.com, and other preferences of your choice.

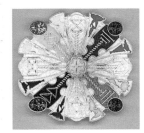

YOUR PUBLIC PROFILE

The page displaying 'Your public profile' is what anyone using www.geocaching.com will see about you. It tells people how long you have been a member, enables them to send you an email message, and includes a section on profile information, the contents of which are entirely at your discretion. You edit the profile information shown on this page by selecting the 'Edit your profile' link near the top of the page.

This page also lists other information.

- **Geocaches**: by selecting the page for 'Geocaches' from within your profile page, you are shown the total number and types of caches you have found, along with any you have created. Select 'All geocache finds' and you will be shown several pages listing all the caches you have found, starting with the most recent. Similarly, if you select 'All geocache hides', you will be shown a list of all the caches you have created.
- **Trackables**: select 'Trackables' from your profile page and you will be shown a list of all the trackable items you have discovered or moved on.
- **Gallery**: the 'Gallery' page shows any photographs you have uploaded to the various cache pages on the website.
- **Bookmark lists**: this page lists any bookmarked lists you may have produced and saved using Pocket Queries.

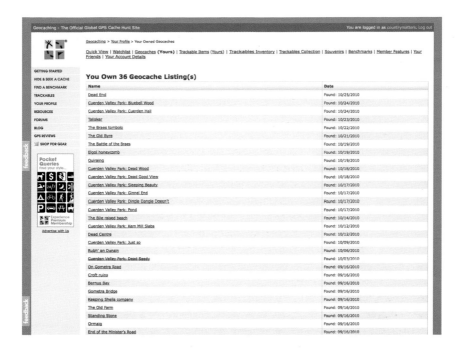

When you first select 'My profile' from the home page, you are shown an abbreviated list of all your logs – found, not found, notes, trackable movements, and so on. By selecting 'Geocaches' from the top menu on this page you are taken to an expanded version of the geocaches you have logged, including your log entry in full. The same is true when you select 'Trackable items'.

Next to each of these links appears (Yours), and by selecting this you are taken to pages displaying your own caches (those you have created) and your own trackable items (any that you have placed and which are originally yours).

These pages enable you quickly to visit your own cache pages, view comments or make changes to the listing.

POCKET QUERIES

Pocket Queries use a system of filters that enable you to search through the database in a specific way, and to have search results emailed to you on a regular basis. Pocket Queries can be especially helpful in planning geocaching trips. Using Pocket Queries, you can receive information about as many as 1000 caches all at one time; many of the modern GPS devices are enabled to accept direct downloads such as these. You can search for caches which meet certain criteria – such as 'dog friendly' or 'recommended

GROUNDSPEAK AND WWW.GEOCACHING.COM

9

for children' – or of a certain type or size. This system also allows you to update the status of any caches you have downloaded so that you can avoid going out in search of caches that have disappeared or have been archived. Only premium members have access to Pocket Queries.

Creating Pocket Queries

The procedure for creating Pocket Queries is lengthy (see below), but not overly complex. Even so, the use of Pocket Queries is something you may want to delay until you have a good understanding of everything that geocaching involves. In this way, you can maximise the benefits that accrue from the use of Pocket Queries.

- On 'Your profile' page, select 'Build Pocket Queries' from the Premium Features in the right-hand menu.
- Select 'Create a new query'.
- On the page headed 'New Pocket Query' give your query a name (such as 'Trackables near home') – something by which you can retrieve it from among any subsequent queries you may create.
- Choose the day of the week on which you want to receive the results of the query.
- Decide how often you would like the query to run. **Note** 'Uncheck the day of the week after the query runs' enables you to run a query once, and then save it in your list of queries for later use.
- Enter the number of cache listings you would like to receive – 1000 is the maximum.
- If you want listings of all types of cache, then leave 'Any type' selected – or you can filter the results by selecting different options.
- If you leave 'Any container' selected, you will get all geocache listings, but you can also filter these selectively.
- Under 'That (And)', leave all boxes unchecked except 'Is active' if you want to receive all live caches, or choose some options to filter the final list.
- To receive caches for all levels of difficulty or terrain, leave the ratings unchecked. Of course, you can select any level of difficulty or terrain.
- Under 'From origin', select the option that gives you the best centre point of the location where you would like to search. You can then enter the radius to delimit an area within which you want to search.
- The greatest number of results will come by leaving unchecked 'Placed during' and 'Attributes'.
- Choose the format in which you want to receive the details. GPX results will give more information, including hints and logs; LOC format gives only co-ordinates.

It is recommended that you select 'Compress files into *.zip format'; GPX and LOC files are text files, and compress very small and download more quickly.

- Select 'Submit information', and the Pocket Query results will be sent to you by email. It may not be an instant response, as the process depends on a dedicated computer handling hundreds of similar requests simultaneously.

- Once you have submitted the information, a 'Preview the search' link appears at the top of the page, on which you can see the results of your search. If you want to make changes to the results, by widening or reducing the search area, for example, then select 'Edit' from the top of the preview page.

POCKET QUERY TIPS

- Queries are generated according to Pacific Standard Time (PST), which is 8 hours behind Greenwich Mean Time (GMT-8). This means that if you generate a query to be produced on a certain day, it could be up to 8 hours before the query runs. What may be Monday in the UK may still be Sunday at Groundspeak HQ.
- The more caches you choose, the larger your query file will be.
- Because you are limited to 1000 caches, in areas densely covered by caches consider using filters to create queries for different types of cache.
- Eliminate caches that you know you are not likely to seek (such as multi- or mystery caches), if you are pressed for time.
- Start with one simple search to see how the system works before creating more. Be sure not to create searches that cannot work, such as EarthCaches with trackable items.

DISCOVER CACHES ALONG A ROUTE

If you are planning to make a long car journey, you can create a query that will find caches along the route, allowing you to stop off and search for caches as you go. Of course, this prolongs the journey immensely, but does make it more interesting. However, the system is highway oriented, and although it can be amended to include deviations, or amended should there be two or more possible routes between the start and finish points, it does not follow public footpaths, and so cannot be used for cross-country routes.

The option to 'Create a route' appears in the right-hand menu of 'Your profile' page. The resultant 'Create/edit a route' page has fields in which you can enter the start and finish points of your journey, and then search. Once you have selected 'Search', you are shown a Google Map depicting your route. Now select 'Save route changes' at the bottom of the page, and you are taken through to a 'Route information' page, in which you can give the route a name, enter a description of the route along with any keywords associated with the route, and then save it. If you tick the box 'Include in public directory', then the route is available for anyone to view.

Other options include 'Modify route' and 'Create a Pocket Query'. Selecting the latter generates a Pocket Query as described above.

Once you have created a route, you can save it, and then revisit it later by selecting 'Find routes' from the right-hand menu on 'Your profile' page.

MANAGE BOOKMARKS

A bookmark list is one defined by you. It can be used to list caches you want to find, to manage your Watchlist, to organise those caches you have found, to create a list that others can follow of caches that may be part of a series, and much more. You can keep the bookmark list private or share it with others.

A bookmark list can be most useful for anyone under-taking, for example, a long-distance trail, who wants to pick up caches along the route. But equally, you can compile a list of, say, your favourite caches, the most difficult caches you encountered, the most remote caches, and so on, and upload them for others to enjoy.

Create a bookmark list

There are a few stages involved in creating a bookmark list, so be sure you want to do it before you make a start.

- From 'Your profile' page, select 'Manage bookmarks' from the right-hand menu.
- On the 'Bookmark lists' page, give your list a name, and select 'Create bookmark list'. On the next page, the name you have given the list is displayed, and you can enter a brief description of the list. Then select 'Create bookmark list'.
- Now you have created a bookmark list, but as yet there is nothing in it. So, go to the first of the caches you want to bookmark, and on the cache page select 'Bookmark listing' from the Navigation panel.
- The next page allows you to create a bookmark, but be

sure to put it in the correct list (from a drop-down menu) if you have created more than one bookmark list.

- Now simply repeat the process until all the caches you want to list are bookmarked.
- Return to 'Manage bookmarks' from the right-hand menu of 'Your profile' page, and you'll be taken through to a page with all your bookmarks listed.
- Select the one you are looking for and click on the hyperlink in the 'Name' column. This now shows all the caches in that particular bookmark, and you can now generate a Pocket Query by selecting 'Create Pocket Query'.

As a final move in this procedure, from your bookmarks list select (right-hand column) 'Download GoogleEarth KML'. This will download Google Earth and overlay on it the locations of all the caches in your bookmark.

INSTANT NOTIFICATIONS

This facility allows you to receive notifications of new caches, in particular event caches near you, but also of caches by type. This is especially useful if all you want to look for are, for example, EarthCaches.

Set up Instant Notifications

- From 'Your profile' page select 'Set up notifications' from the right-hand menu. Then select 'Create a new notification'.
- Give your notification a name – such as 'New caches' – and then choose a type of cache to watch by selecting from a drop-down menu – such as 'Traditional cache'.
- An additional list now appears with 10 options. If you want to receive only notifications of new caches, simply select 'Publish listing'.
- You need to select the co-ordinates which form the centre of the cache search area. This will default to your home co-ordinates, but you can reset it to a new location if you are searching for caches away from your home location. If you have not yet set your home co-ordinates, see Chapter 3.
- Set the distance from your home co-ordinates that you want to receive information about, for example 10km.
- Check 'Enable notifications'.
- Select 'Create notification'.

You will now receive an email every time a new cache meeting your criteria is published. If you want more than one type of cache, then set up multiple notifications.

Whitby Bay is the location of a number of caches linked to Bram Stoker, creator of Frankenstein

10 EVENTS, ACTIVITIES AND MORE ADVANCED STUFF

This final chapter rounds up a wide range of miscellaneous topics, all of which are relevant to the pursuit of geocaching in some way. While the activities are all incidental to the core activity of geocaching, becoming involved in one or more of them will only serve to enhance the experience.

Geocaching is a worldwide activity – only about 60,000 of the 1.2 million caches are in the UK. Searching for caches in other countries is exactly the same as in the UK (but see Chapter 5, 'Search strategies', on using downloaded GPS co-ordinates overseas), although there is no guarantee that the cache page contents will be in English – you may have to resort to Google Translation to figure out the clues. The weekly Groundspeak newsletter contains information about event caches worldwide, enabling you to meet with other geocachers while on holiday!

CACHE IN TRASH OUT

Cache In Trash Out (CITO) is an ongoing environmental initiative supported by the worldwide geocaching community. Since 2002, geocachers have sought to clean up parks and other cache-friendly places around the world. All events are organised by volunteers and help preserve the natural beauty of our countryside.

Annually, Groundspeak celebrates international CITO events where geocachers have an opportunity to participate in co-ordinated worldwide clean-up efforts. Geocachers host CITO events in their local area on the same day or weekend as other geocachers around the world. Together, these events make an enormous positive impact and generate a lot of fun for the participants in the process. With the permission of CADW (the historic environment service of the Welsh government), the UK's first CITO event took place at Flint Castle, Flintshire, Wales, in July 2004, with a get-together featuring a buffet after the event.

GETTING INVOLVED, HAVING FUN AND JOINING A LOCAL ORGANISATION

Geocaching can be very much a solitary endeavour. Yet there is considerable pleasure from getting involved with other geocachers in your own area. If local events are organised, then they become an 'event cache', at which

A group of geocachers set off across Morecambe Bay with Queen's Guide Cedric Robinson MBE as part of an event cache

your attendance scores you a point in your overall tally of caches found. The easiest way to find out about events in your area is to set up an Instant Notification (see Chapter 9), selecting 'Event caches'. In this way, you can be sure that as soon as an event is published, you will receive an email telling you about it.

Geocaching events are popular social occasions, and some may involve a quick bout of geocaching followed by a convivial evening in a local pub. Others may be timed to coincide with, for example, the twice-yearly equinoxes or some historical event of local significance. Or they might take the form of a few hours' birdwatching at a local reserve, or the celebration of someone's birthday or other significant event. The range of possibilities is limited only by imagination.

One of the ways you can enhance your geocaching experience is to join a local group. These are not widespread across the UK, but currently are strongest in the north-west of England and the south-east; others certainly will evolve. The north-west geocaching group can be contacted through www.nwcaching.co.uk; the south-east group through www. secaching.co.uk.

Both of these organisations have website forums on which you can pose questions, raise issues or simply ask for advice about GPS devices, techniques, equipment, and so on, or even about difficult caches. There are a number of other groups and forums from which you can glean information

- Yorkshire Geocaching: www.yorkshiregeocaching.co.uk
- GeoX (Geo for Grown-ups): www.geox.easyphpbb.com/index.php
- Geofrees (Geocaching Scotland): www.geofrees.org/Forum/
- South Wales Geocaching, 'Geogelcwyr de Cymru': www.southwalesgeocachers.co.uk/forum/index.php
- emCache (East Midlands Geocaching): www.emcache.com/ (this is also the forum home for iCache, a Groundspeak-approved and -supported UK stats site)
- EACachers (East Anglian Cachers): www.eacachers.org.uk/

Groundspeak also has a range of forums, which have a worldwide audience. They can be accessed via 'Forums' in the left-hand column of the www.geocaching.com home page.

GEOCACHING ASSOCIATION OF GREAT BRITAIN

The Geocaching Association of Great Britain

www.gagb.org.uk

(logo reproduced with permision)

The Geocaching Association of Great Britain (GAGB) was set up by a group of experienced geocachers in response to a perceived need for an association to represent the geocaching community in the UK at a national level, to enhance geocaching in the UK, and to facilitate its progress.

It does this by:

- liaising with local and national land-owning bodies, and agreeing guidelines so that caching on their land is approved and encouraged
- helping all associates to enjoy the activity without falling foul of the civil and criminal laws of the land
- establishing good caching practices by accepting advice from land, environmental, archaeological and historical bodies
- acting as an intermediary and as the first point of call for all interested parties in Great Britain
- ensuring that the positive educational, environmental and recreational aspects of geocaching are properly represented
- helping new members of the geocaching community when they begin.

The Association:

- negotiates with major owners of publicly accessible land in Great Britain for a positive approach to geocaching
- encourages appropriate publicity to promote geocaching

10

Geocaching is fun for all the family

- maintains a page of links to websites containing information on environmental, legal and other topics of interest to geocachers
- has developed a definitive set of geocaching guidelines specific to Great Britain
- has developed a reference system to summarise laws and other issues which impact on geocaching in Great Britain.

Over the years, the Association has negotiated the majority of the agreements with major land-owner for permission to carry out geocaching on their land. A list of all landowners who allow geocaching, and those who have banned geocaching, appears on its website (www.gagb.co.uk). Some, but not all, of these landowners require you to get permission using a specific application form. The website has downloadable application forms to be completed before the relevant landowners will consider access.

WWW.OPENCACHING.ORG.UK

The website www.geocaching.com is not the only geocaching database. Although as yet of limited extent, www.opencaching.org.uk is a UK-specific database that operates on similar principles to www.geocaching.com, but is confined to caches located in the UK. There are similar opencaching sites in Finland, Germany, Poland and the Czech Republic (www.opencaching.eu), as well as Australia, Hungary, Estonia, Rumania, Turkey and Russia.

MERCHANDISING

Groundspeak has an online 'shop' selling a wide range of geocaching products. It is accessible from the www. geocaching.com home page via 'Shop for gear'. (This book gives a list of UK online outlets in Appendix C.)

BENCHMARKING

Benchmarks are vertical control stations used by Ordnance Survey for measuring elevation, and their position is known by Ordnance Survey to a high degree of accuracy. The search for benchmarks is an add-on activity allied to geocaching. The development of searches for benchmarks originated in the US, and much of the information on the www.geocaching.com website is US related. But it is an additional and moderate interest that can be pursued by geocachers in the UK.

Benchmarks in the UK are most noticeable in two forms – a cut benchmark engraved into stone, and the same shaped embossed into a small bracket (known as a flush bracket) affixed to the base of Ordnance Survey trig pillars, which carry a unique identifying number (S1543, for example, is the trig-pillar bracket on the summit of Skiddaw in the Lake District).

Flush brackets were first used during the Second Geodetic Levelling of England and Wales (2GL) between 1912 and 1921. The 2GL brackets were numbered 1 to 3000, and the vast majority of these brackets were placed on walls and buildings, with only a small number (only 46, in the range 2943 to 2999) being affixed to triangulation pillars. There is a greater number of a different type of bracket, known as S-brackets because they are prefixed with the letter 'S'. These range from S01 to S9999, and were introduced in 1920. This series also includes a number of brackets numbered 10,000 and higher but without the 'S' prefix. A G-series of flush brackets first appeared in 1936, at the commencement of the Second Geodetic Levelling of Scotland. G-series brackets are found exclusively on walls. Finally, a small series of just 16 brackets, the L-series (L1 to L16), was affixed during the Re-levelling of Greater London from 1931 to 1934.

Benchmarks can be found at various locations all over the UK, and you can discover UK benchmarks via the Ordnance Survey Bench Mark Database at www.benchmarks.org.uk. You can search locally by using your post code. Go to the website and enter your postcode into the 'Search' box, and a list will appear of benchmarks near you. Or you can select 'Search' from the header menu of the database and define the type of benchmarks you are

S-series flush bracket

Bolt benchmark

Cut benchmark

EVENTS, ACTIVITIES AND MORE ADVANCED STUFF

10

looking for. Your benchmark finds can be logged on www.
waymarking.com.

WAYMARKING

Waymarking is similar to geocaching, but with waymarking there are no physical cache containers. The pursuit centres around points of interest, such as buildings, vehicles, monuments, signs, structures (such as canal bridges), mountain summits, places of recreation or entertainment, and even weird story locations. Given this width of potential, it is clear that there are thousands of waymarks across the UK.

Historically, what are today known as 'waymarks' used to be loggable on www.geocaching.com in the category 'Locationless reverse' (such as GCCF43). But this category is no longer used. Locationless caches are the opposite of a traditional cache. Instead of finding a hidden container, you are given a task to locate a specific object and log its coordinates. In about 2005, Groundspeak decided to archive all locationless caches, but as a result all these caches became categories on a website dedicated to waymarking, www.waymarking.com, and the pursuit of waymarking started from there. You can use this website to discover the waymarks near you.

Cadair Idris in Snowdonia has a typical summit cache

SUMMIT CACHING

These caches were originally created by and for radio amateurs taking part in the 'Summits of the Air' (SOTA) programme. Numerous hill summits in Britain were catalogued, and radio hams 'activated' them by transmitting from the summits. But because of the difficulty of carrying radio equipment to the top of a hill, it was decided to create conventional caches on some (but not all) summits. Radio hams could now obtain credit for finding them as official geocaches, rather than needing to transmit from the summit. And because they are physical caches, they can be searched for by geocachers too.

The summit caching website – www.summitcaching.org. uk – includes summit tables, showing the number of finders of each 'cache', along with annual and overall league tables, should you wish to join in this pursuit. As the caches are hidden on mountain tops, geocachers who are hill walkers will find this an interesting addition to the basic pursuit of geocaching. Some are easy to find and some are hard, especially under winter conditions and bad weather. This activity is independent of and not an official part of the SOTA programme.

Summits where it has not been possible to place a geocache, perhaps because there is already a geocache in close proximity, have been registered as waymarks (see above).

TRIGPOINTING

Trigpoints – a familiar name for triangulation pillars – are the Ordnance Survey obelisks dotted around the countryside. These concrete pillars, about 4ft tall, were used by the Ordnance Survey to survey the landscape of the country in order to create detailed maps. They are usually, but not exclusively, located on the highest point of ground in an area, so that there is a direct line of sight from one to the next. By sitting a theodolite (an accurate compass built into a telescope) on the top of the pillar, exact bearings to nearby trigpoints could be taken. No longer required for active service, many trigpoints have been adopted by individuals, who have taken over responsibility for their upkeep. Each of these 'trigs' originally had what is known as a flush bracket – a metal plate, attached to the pillar, carrying a unique reference number and a benchmark.

The practice of 'bagging' trigpoints is another add-on feature of geocaching. The search for many geocaches will lead you past trigpoints, so it becomes a logical extension of geocaching to make a note of the numbers on trig pillars, and then to log them on www.trigpointinguk.com, a dedicated website. However, bear in mind that many trigpoints

10

are on private land to which there is no access other than by courtesy of the land owner.

CACHE STATISTICS

The geocaching website hosts all the information about caches that you have found or placed. But as the number of caches you discover increases, keeping track of those that you were the first to find, or those of varying levels of difficulty and terrain, becomes complicated. But there are a few ways in which all this data can be harnessed and collated in a meaningful way.

You begin by creating a Pocket Query, as described in Chapter 9, but selecting 'I have found' under the panel curiously named 'That (And)'. You can call the query 'My finds' or something similar. Once you have created a Pocket Query you can run it by adding it to the queue, and then waiting for the result to arrive by email. The results of the query will arrive as a zip file, so you will need WinZip or similar software to open it. But first, before opening the zip file, save it to your computer.

Downloaded zip files should automatically be directed to the 'Unzipped' folder in your 'Downloads' folder. But, in addition, save a copy of the unopened zip file to your geocaching folder.

On your computer create a folder called 'Geocaching', and get into the habit of placing anything relating to geocaching in there.

Now you need to download software (free) that will manage the data from the Pocket Query. Cachestats is one format, and this is downloadable from www.logicweave.com.

Having downloaded the data management software, you now need to give it the data from the Pocket Query to manipulate.

- **Cachestats**: unzip the zip file. This creates a GPX file. Your computer will automatically place this in the 'Unzipped' folder, but you may want to redirect it to your geocaching folder, and you will be given the opportunity to do this during the unzipping process. Now run the Cachestats software, during the course of which you will be asked to 'Open a GPX file'. Use this to locate and open the file, and the software will then produce tables of statistics that show your progress, including yearly data, a calendar of your geocaching activity, significant milestones, locations, size/type of caches found, difficult and terrain and a D/T square (see below).

D/T SQUARES

Geocaching, if you haven't realised it by now, is about challenges. One particular form of challenge is to find caches that meet every combination of difficulty and terrain. This is shown on a D/T square, sometimes also called a 9x9 grid or a D/T grid.

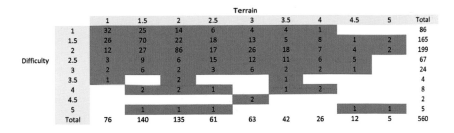

		Terrain								
		1	1.5	2	2.5	3	3.5	4	4.5	5	Total
Difficulty	1	32	25	14	6	4	4	1			86
	1.5	26	70	22	18	13	5	8	1	2	165
	2	12	27	86	17	26	18	7	4	2	199
	2.5	3	9	6	15	12	11	6	5		67
	3	2	6	2	3	6	2	2	1		24
	3.5	1		2			1				4
	4		2	2	1		1	2			8
	4.5					2					2
	5		1	1	1				1	1	5
	Total	76	140	135	61	63	42	26	12	5	560

The object of the D/T square, of course, is to complete it, something that most geocachers do in part. But finding the most difficult caches is a challenge in itself. There are even a few caches, such as GC1JTG4, that you can find only when you've completed the D/T square. It's all part of the fun.

A typical D/T square

EARTHCACHE MASTER PROGRAMME
The EarthCache element of geocaching is designed to help people to understand the Earth in a geological context. Seeking out EarthCaches is an opportunity for all the family to learn something about the landscape and its creation. The listing of EarthCache sites is done by the Geological Society of America.

EARTHCACHE MASTER
BRONZE LEVEL

As part of the process of acquiring EarthCaches, you have the chance to become part of the EarthCache Master's programme. There are four EarthCache Master levels: bronze, silver, gold and platinum.

- **Bronze EarthCache Master**: you must visit and log 3 or more EarthCaches in 2 or more countries (Scotland, England, Wales and Northern Ireland count as separate countries for this purpose).
- **Silver EarthCache Master**: visit and log 6 or more EarthCaches in 3 or more countries, and develop 1 or more EarthCaches of your own.
- **Gold EarthCache Master**: visit and log 12 or more EarthCaches in 4 or more countries, and develop 2 or more EarthCaches.
- **Platinum EarthCache Master**: visit and log 20 or more EarthCaches in 5 or more countries, and develop 3 or more EarthCaches.

Information about EarthCaches can be found at www.earthcache.org, run by the organisation to which you submit your claims to the different levels of membership.

EVENTS, ACTIVITIES AND MORE ADVANCED STUFF

10

109

GEOCACHING CO-ORDINATES CHECKER

If you place a cache that requires someone to solve a puzzle before arriving at the correct co-ordinates, you can use www.geochecker.com to allow people to check that they have correctly solved the puzzle. As a cache owner, you enter the cache name and cache code along with the correct co-ordinates. Then you create a code, which links to your cache page and allows puzzle solvers to check their work.

This website also lists the 25 most popular puzzles, along with the 25 hardest puzzles (not all of them in the UK).

GEOCACHING SWISS ARMY KNIFE

The Geocaching Swiss Army Knife (GSAK) is an all-in-one geocaching and waypoint management tool. Major features include – multiple databases, sending/receiving waypoints to GPS, Google Maps, conversion to many mapping formats, iPhone/Blackberry output (including CacheMate support), HTML output, extensive searching, macro support, backup and restore, distance/direction from other waypoints (including caches, locations, post codes) and much more. GSAK runs only on Windows operating systems (98, ME, NT, 2000, XP, Vista, Windows 7).

GSAK is a more sophisticated version of cache statistic programs, and has much greater functionality. Its various complexities, however, are likely to prove of benefit only to geocachers who have established a good level of understanding of the way geocaching works. Once achieved, the benefits of GSAK can be more readily understood. It is beyond the scope of this book to explain the whole range of GSAK possibilities, but the software is available from www.gsak.net. There is a free version, although the cost of registering for a paid version is nominal.

Appendix A
UNDERSTANDING GEO-SPEAK

As with many activities, a dedicated language has evolved for geocaching, much of it abbreviated to initial letters. The language is evolving all the time. Here is a basic glossary of terms.

archived: describes a cache that no longer exists (for a variety of reasons), but which still appears in the database for historical purposes. A cache might be archived because it has been lost, is no longer maintained by the owner, or does not abide by the guidelines determining where and how caches may be placed.

cache and dash: (*aka* drive-by) is a cache that is placed close to a convenient parking spot, from which you can quickly dash to the cache location

CITO: Cache In Trash Out

DNF: 'Did not find'. Using DNF when you log your search on www.geocaching.com records the fact that you were unable to find the cache. It also alerts the owner to the possibility that the cache may be missing.

drive-by: see 'cache and dash'

event cache: a formal or informal get-together of geocachers, which may range from a pie and a pint in a pub to an organised collective search for caches or a multi-day event

FTF: 'First to find'. A simple message entered in the log by the first person to find a cache. Sometimes 2TF ('Second to find') is also used, but after that it becomes meaningless.

GC code: cache code

GPS: Global Positioning System (system of satellites) or a GPS device

GZ: Ground Zero. The spot where the cache co-ordinates and those on your GPS are a match. Note, however,

that the cache may not always be at GZ because the co-ordinates may be out by a small amount.

hitchhiker: an object that moves from cache to cache, marked with some instructions, telling the finder what to do with it; also known as a **traveller**

muggle: a term borrowed from the Harry Potter books to refer to people who are not geocachers

PAF: 'Phone a friend'. PAF signifies that the cache was difficult to find, and that the finder succeeded only by telephoning another geocacher who had already found the cache. This is done not so much to receive the exact whereabouts of the cache, but to get additional information or help. Also **TAF**: 'Text a friend'.

SL: 'Signed log'. Entered on the website to signify that the finder signed the log contained in the cache

spoiler: information or a photograph that might give away the exact location of a cache

TFTC: 'Thanks for the cache'. A courtesy note left when logging a find on the website.

TNLN: 'Took nothing, left nothing'. Note left on the website that signifies that the finder took nothing from the cache and placed nothing in it. Many finders enter 'TFTC TNLN SL' on the website.

waypoint: a location, expressed in the same format as cache co-ordinates, that relates not to the cache itself but to a useful feature – such as a convenient car park or a bridge – that you might need in order to reach the cache location

Appendix B
THE GEOCACHER'S CODE

The Geocacher's Code is designed to help orient new players to the ethos of the geocaching community and to guide experienced players in questionable situations, so that everyone can enjoy geocaching!

The articles of the code are set out below in bold. Underneath each are several examples of how to apply the code in real-life situations. (These are examples only and not part of the code.) Of course, not every contingency can be spelled out, so if a specific situation is not covered in the examples, you should consider the intent expressed in the main articles in making a decision.

I will avoid endangering myself or others.

- Like any outdoor activity, geocaching involves some inherent risk, and many geocachers enjoy manageable risks. Minimise inordinate risks.
- When creating a cache, describe any hidden dangers and, if possible, arrange the hunt to minimise these dangers.
- When seeking a cache, know your limitations and be aware of your surroundings. Don't attempt anything beyond your abilities.
- A cache you own, or one you're trading out of, could be found by children – consider the location of the cache and those likely to find it when deciding what to leave as a trade item.

Observe all laws and rules of the area

- Don't break the law or rules of an area, or encourage others to do so, when placing or seeking a cache.
- Don't leave illegal items in a cache.

Respect property rights and seek permission where appropriate

- Check if permission is required before placing a cache on private property, and respect the landowner's wishes.
- Check if public land has a geocaching policy, and respect existing policies.
- Promptly remove your cache if the land manager asks.
- Do not damage, or interfere with the function of, buildings, structures or signage.

Avoid causing disruption or public alarm

- Don't place a cache near schools or government buildings unless the administration and staff are fully aware of the placement.
- Use caution where children play. Parents are understandably concerned when strangers are near their children.
- Don't place a cache near critical infrastructure that might be considered a terrorist target, or create a cache that could be mistaken for a terrorist device.

I will minimise my own and others' impact on the environment.

- Follow 'Leave No Trace' ethics whenever possible.
- When seeking a cache, practise 'Lift, Look, Replace'. Put all stones or logs back where you found them. Leave the area as you found it or better (eg pick up litter).
- Obtain the best possible co-ordinates for your cache to reduce unwarranted wear on the area. Recheck and correct your co-ordinates if finders report significant errors.
- Do not abandon a cache.
- If you stop maintaining a cache, remove the container, archive its listing (using the option in the Navigation panel on the relevant cache page) and explain the disposition of the cache in your archive note, or put it up for adoption or rescue by writing a note as a log entry.

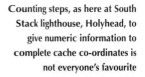

Counting steps, as here at South Stack lighthouse, Holyhead, to give numeric information to complete cache co-ordinates is not everyone's favourite

I will be considerate of others.

- Treat other geocachers civilly – in the field, in forums, or wherever your paths may cross.
- Don't spoil the hunt for others – allow them to experience the cache as its owner intended.
- Avoid leaving tracks to the cache. Do not disrupt the cache area or mark the hiding spot.
- Minimise giving unsolicited clues that reveal the cache ('spoilers').
- Don't provide any hints if the cache description asks you not to. In all other cases, be cryptic or encrypt any hints or spoilers you enter in online logs.
- Edit your log if the cache owner requests that you remove spoilers.
- Promptly alert the owner of any issues with their cache. Make minor repairs if you can – it will save the owner a trip.
- Cache owners appreciate feedback – write an online log, send an email, or otherwise let the owner know about your experience with their cache.
- Only place caches you can maintain and respond promptly to problem reports.
- If you exchange trade items, trade kindly – consider what future finders would like, and leave something equal to or better than what you take.

'Barnaby in the wild' – geocaching is a great way to encourage children to appreciate our countryside (photo: Mark Fishwick)

- If you place a travelling item into the game, attach a tag that describes its goal, so that others can help it along. If you pick up a travelling item with a tag describing its goal, move the item towards its goal if possible. Contact the owner if you hold a travelling item for more than a couple of weeks or so.
- Obtain permission from the originator before copying unique themes and techniques, adding to an existing series of caches, or placing a cache close to another.

I wil protect the integrity of the game pieces.

- The owner trusts you to not damage or jeopardise the cache. Try to ensure that the cache is ready for the next finder, and is as good as or better than when you found it.
- Make sure the container is properly closed to prevent the contents from getting wet or destroyed.
- Be inconspicuous in retrieving, signing in, and replacing a cache to avoid vandalism.
- Put the cache back where you found it and hide it well. Don't move a cache – if you suspect the cache is not in the intended spot, hide it as well as you can and alert the owner as soon as possible.
- Don't collect travelling items meant to stay in the game. This is theft.
- Don't tamper with or involve a game piece in 'alternate' games without the owner's permission.

Appendix C
THE NATIONAL COUNTRY CODES

England, Wales and Scotland each have their own official codes outlining the responsibilities of anyone enjoying the countryside, whether it be national parks, access land or common land and these codes express the same general principles. The points below are a summary of the Countryside Code for England.

- **Be safe – plan ahead and follow any signs**
  Even when going out locally, it's best to get the latest information about where and when you can go; for example, your rights to go onto some areas of open land may be restricted while work is carried out, for safety reasons or during breeding seasons. Follow advice and local signs, and be prepared for the unexpected.
- **Protect plants and animals, and take your litter home**
  We have a responsibility to protect our countryside now and future generations, so make sure you don't harm animals, birds, plants, or trees.
- **Keep dogs under close control**
  The countryside is a great place to exercise dogs, but it's every owner's duty to make sure their dog is not a danger or nuisance to farm animals, wildlife or other people.
- **Leave gates and property as you find them**
  Please respect the working life of the countryside, as our actions can affect people's livelihoods, our heritage, and the safety and welfare of animals and ourselves.
- **Consider other people**
  Showing consideration and respect for other people makes the countryside a pleasant environment for everyone – at home, at work and at leisure.

The full version of the Countryside Code for England is available online at www.countrysideaccess.gov.uk.

The Welsh Countryside Code is available at www.countrysidecodewales.org.uk and the Scottish Outdoor Access Code is available at www.outdooraccess-scotland.com. There is no official code for Ireland but Leave no Trace Ireland outdoor ethics programme promotes a similar ethos in its 'seven principles' available at www.leavenotrace ireland.org.

'Under a rock', Isle of Skye

Appendix D
ACCESS TO THE COUNTRYSIDE: WALKERS AND THE LAW

Geocaching in the UK can take place almost anywhere, from town centres to remote mountain tops, although there tend to be restrictions, or at least careful control, over the placement of geocaches in environmentally sensitive areas, and other places where there is an actual or perceived danger. The guidelines for placing caches are contained elsewhere but the opportunity is taken here to give a brief summary of the law of access, that is the freedom to roam, particularly as it applies to the open countryside, although this is not a definitive statement of the law.

The mere fact that a cache exists does not mean that you have access to it other than within the law; in other words, you are not at liberty to commit a trespass or cause damage in pursuit of a cache. You have to get there lawfully.

ENGLAND AND WALES

The law relating to access in England and Wales is enshrined in the Countryside and Rights of Way Act, 2000, usually shortened to the 'CRoW Act, 2000'.

Until the passing of the CRoW Act, walkers could legally access the countryside only along rights of way: public footpaths, bridleways, and Byways Open to All Traffic (BOATs). The CRoW Act amended existing legislation and provides for access on foot to certain categories of land, notably mountain, moor, heath, down and common land. In effect, this means that walkers now have access to large areas of open land. There is no restriction on continuing to use existing rights of way, but the difference is that you may now leave the right of way and wander freely, but only within those areas designated as Access Land. These are shown on Ordnance Survey maps by a yellow tint within a pale orange border.

This freedom to roam gives geocachers the opportunity to place caches in remote locations, and they frequently do, often far from convenient paths. In this respect geocachers differ from recreational walkers, not least because existing pathways follow the driest and surest routes across land; the fact that you can wander anywhere on Access Land is not always the benefit it may seem.

SCOTLAND

The situation in Scotland is slightly different. Here, walkers have always taken access, by custom, tradition or right, over most land. The law in Scotland is now embodied in the Land Reform (Scotland) Act, 2003, which came into effect in February 2005.

The Land Reform (Scotland) Act, 2003 tells you where rights of access apply in Scotland, while the Scottish Outdoor Access Code sets out your responsibilities when exercising your rights. These responsibilities can be summarised as:

* take responsibility for your own actions
* respect the interests of other people, and
* care for the environment.

Access rights can be exercised over most land and inland water in Scotland by all non-motorised users, including walkers, cyclists, horse riders and canoeists, providing they do so responsibly. Walkers and others must behave in ways which are compatible with land management needs, and land managers also have reciprocal responsibilities to manage their land to facilitate access, taken either by right, custom or tradition. Local authorities and national park authorities have a duty and the powers to uphold access rights.

People may be requested not to take access for certain periods of time when, for example, tree-felling is taking place, during the stalking season, or for nature conservation reasons. It is responsible to comply with reasonable requests. Access rights also extend to lightweight, informal camping.

Farmyards are not included in the right of access, but you may still take access through farmyards by rights-of-way, custom or tradition. Farmers are encouraged to sign alternative routes if they do not want people passing through their farmyard. If you are going through a farmyard, proceed with care and respect the privacy of those living on the farm.

NORTHERN IRELAND

Northern Ireland has very few public rights of way and therefore in many areas walkers enjoy the countryside only by the goodwill and tolerance of landowners.

Much of Northern Ireland's public land, such as Water Service and Forest Service land, is also accessible, as is land owned and managed by organisations such as the National Trust and the Woodland Trust.

Appendix E
ONLINE SUPPLIERS IN THE UK

Above & Beyond
Tel: 0800 112 3010
Email: biz@aboveandbeyond.co.uk
www.aboveandbeyond.co.uk

Cache Zone
www.cachezone.co.uk

eXpansys UK Limited
Tel: 0161 868 0868;
www.expansys.com

Finger Technology Limited
Tel: 01923 289878
Email: info@fingertech.co.uk;
www.fingertech.co.uk

Geotastic
Tel:0844 887 0652
www.geotastic.com

Geotees
www.geotees.co.uk and www.geotees.eu

Geotogs
www.shop.geotogs.com

UKGeocache
www.ukgeocache.com

UKGeocachers
Tel: 01335 301266
Email: admin@ukgeocachers.co.uk
www.ukgeocachers.co.uk

Skyblue Leisure
Tel: 01637 852775
www.skyblueleisure.co.uk

The Geocaching Shop
www.thegeocachingshop.com

INDEX

LISTING OF CICERONE GUIDES

BRITISH ISLES CHALLENGES, COLLECTIONS AND ACTIVITIES
The End to End Trail
The Mountains of England and Wales
1 Wales
2 England
The National Trails
The Relative Hills of Britain
The Ridges of England, Wales and Ireland
The UK Trailwalker's Handbook
Three Peaks, Ten Tors

MOUNTAIN LITERATURE
Unjustifiable Risk?

UK CYCLING
Border Country Cycle Routes
Cycling in the Peak District
Lands End to John O'Groats Cycle Guide
Mountain Biking in the Lake District
The Lancashire Cycleway

SCOTLAND
Backpacker's Britain
Central and Southern Scottish Highlands
Northern Scotland
Ben Nevis and Glen Coe
North to the Cape
Not the West Highland Way
Scotland's Best Small Mountains
Scotland's Far West
Scotland's Mountain Ridges
Scrambles in Lochaber
The Border Country
The Central Highlands
The Great Glen Way
The Isle of Mull
The Isle of Skye
The Pentland Hills: A Walker's Guide
The Southern Upland Way
The Speyside Way
The West Highland Way
Walking in Scotland's Far North
Walking in the Cairngorms
Walking in the Hebrides
Walking in the Ochils, Campsie Fells and Lomond Hills
Walking in Torridon
Walking Loch Lomond and the Trossachs
Walking on Harris and Lewis
Walking on Jura, Islay and Colonsay
Walking on the Isle of Arran
Walking on the Orkney and Shetland Isles
Walking the Galloway Hills
Walking the Lowther Hills
Walking the Munros
1 Southern, Central and Western Highlands
2 Northern Highlands and the Cairngorms

Winter Climbs Ben Nevis and Glen Coe
Winter Climbs in the Cairngorms
World Mountain Ranges: Scotland

NORTHERN ENGLAND TRAILS
A Northern Coast to Coast Walk
Backpacker's Britain
Northern England
Hadrian's Wall Path
The Dales Way
The Pennine Way
The Spirit of Hadrian's Wall

NORTH EAST ENGLAND, YORKSHIRE DALES AND PENNINES
Historic Walks in North Yorkshire
South Pennine Walks
The Cleveland Way and the Yorkshire Wolds Way
The North York Moors
The Reivers Way
The Teesdale Way
The Yorkshire Dales Angler's Guide
The Yorkshire Dales
North and East
South and West
Walking in County Durham
Walking in Northumberland
Walking in the North Pennines
Walking in the Wolds
Walks in Dales Country
Walks in the Yorkshire Dales
Walks on the North York Moors
Books 1 & 2

NORTH WEST ENGLAND AND THE ISLE OF MAN
A Walker's Guide to the Lancaster Canal
Historic Walks in Cheshire
Isle of Man Coastal Path
The Isle of Man
The Ribble Way
Walking in Lancashire
Walking in the Forest of Bowland and Pendle
Walking on the West Pennine Moors
Walks in Lancashire Witch Country
Walks in Ribble Country
Walks in Silverdale and Arnside
Walks in the Forest of Bowland

LAKE DISTRICT
Coniston Copper Mines
Great Mountain Days in the Lake District
Lake District Winter Climbs
Lakeland Fellranger
The Central Fells
The Mid-Western Fells
The Near Eastern Fells
The Southern Fells

Roads and Tracks of the Lake District
Rocky Rambler's Wild Walks
Scrambles in the Lake District
North & South
Short Walks in Lakeland
1 South Lakeland
2 North Lakeland
3 West Lakeland
The Cumbria Coastal Way
The Cumbria Way and the Allerdale Ramble
The Lake District Anglers' Guide
Tour of the Lake District

DERBYSHIRE, PEAK DISTRICT AND MIDLANDS
High Peak Walks
The Star Family Walks
Walking in Derbyshire
White Peak Walks
The Northern Dales
The Southern Dales

SOUTHERN ENGLAND
A Walker's Guide to the Isle of Wight
London – The definitive walking guide
The Cotswold Way
The Greater Ridgeway
The Lea Valley Walk
The North Downs Way
The South Downs Way
The South West Coast Path
The Thames Path
Walking in Bedfordshire
Walking in Berkshire
Walking in Buckinghamshire
Walking in Kent
Walking in Sussex
Walking in the Isles of Scilly
Walking in the Thames Valley
Walking on Dartmoor

WALES AND WELSH BORDERS
Backpacker's Britain
Wales
Glyndwr's Way
Great Mountain Days in Snowdonia
Hillwalking in Snowdonia
Hillwalking in Wales
Vols 1 & 2
Offa's Dyke Path
Ridges of Snowdonia
Scrambles in Snowdonia
The Ascent of Snowdon
The Lleyn Peninsula Coastal Path
The Pembrokeshire Coastal Path
The Shropshire Hills
The Spirit Paths of Wales
Walking in Pembrokeshire
Walking on the Brecon Beacons
Welsh Winter Climbs

INTERNATIONAL CHALLENGES, COLLECTIONS AND ACTIVITIES
Canyoning
Europe's High Points

EUROPEAN CYCLING
Cycle Touring in France
Cycle Touring in Ireland
Cycle Touring in Spain
Cycle Touring in Switzerland
Cycling in the French Alps
Cycling the Canal du Midi
Cycling the River Loire
The Danube Cycleway
The Grand Traverse of the
  Massif Central
The Way of St James

AFRICA
Climbing in the Moroccan Anti-
  Atlas
Kilimanjaro: A Complete
  Trekker's Guide
Mountaineering in the
  Moroccan High Atlas
Trekking in the Atlas Mountains
Walking in the Drakensberg

ALPS – CROSS-BORDER ROUTES
100 Hut Walks in the Alps
Across the Eastern Alps: E5
Alpine Ski Mountaineering
  1 Western Alps
  2 Central and Eastern Alps
Chamonix to Zermatt
Snowshoeing
Tour of Mont Blanc
Tour of Monte Rosa
Tour of the Matterhorn
Walking in the Alps
Walks and Treks in the Maritime
  Alps

PYRENEES AND FRANCE/SPAIN CROSS-BORDER ROUTES
Rock Climbs In The Pyrenees
The GR10 Trail
The Mountains of Andorra
The Pyrenean Haute Route
The Pyrenees
The Way of St James
  France & Spain
Through the Spanish Pyrenees:
  GR11
Walks and Climbs in the
  Pyrenees

AUSTRIA
Trekking in Austria's Hohe
  Tauern
Trekking in the Stubai Alps
Trekking in the Zillertal Alps
Walking in Austria

EASTERN EUROPE
The High Tatras
The Mountains of Romania
Walking in Bulgaria's National
  Parks
Walking in Hungary

FRANCE
Ecrins National Park
GR20: Corsica
Mont Blanc Walks
The Cathar Way

The GR5 Trail
The Robert Louis Stevenson
  Trail
Tour of the Oisans: The GR54
Tour of the Queyras
Tour of the Vanoise
Trekking in the Vosges and Jura
Vanoise Ski Touring
Walking in Provence
Walking in the Cathar Region
Walking in the Cevennes
Walking in the Dordogne
Walking in the Haute Savoie
  North & South
Walking in the Languedoc
Walking in the Tarentaise and
  Beaufortain Alps
Walking on Corsica

GERMANY
Germany's Romantic Road
Walking in the Bavarian Alps
Walking in the Harz Mountains
Walking the River Rhine Trail

HIMALAYA
Annapurna: A Trekker's Guide
Bhutan
Everest: A Trekker's Guide
Garhwal and Kumaon: A
  Trekker's and Visitor's Guide
Kangchenjunga: A Trekker's
  Guide
Langtang with Gosainkund and
  Helambu: A Trekker's Guide
Manaslu: A Trekker's Guide
The Mount Kailash Trek

IRELAND
Irish Coastal Walks
The Irish Coast to Coast Walk
The Mountains of Ireland

ITALY
Gran Paradiso
Italy's Sibillini National Park
Shorter Walks in the Dolomites
Through the Italian Alps
Trekking in the Apennines
Trekking in the Dolomites
Via Ferratas of the Italian
  Dolomites: Vols 1 & 2
Walking in Sicily
Walking in the Central Italian
  Alps
Walking in the Dolomites
Walking in Tuscany
Walking on the Amalfi Coast

MEDITERRANEAN
Jordan – Walks, Treks, Caves,
  Climbs and Canyons
The Ala Dag
The High Mountains of Crete
The Mountains of Greece
Treks and Climbs in Wadi Rum,
  Jordan
Walking in Malta
Western Crete

NORTH AMERICA
British Columbia
The Grand Canyon
The John Muir Trail
The Pacific Crest Trail

SOUTH AMERICA
Aconcagua and the Southern
  Andes
Torres del Paine

SCANDINAVIA
Trekking in Greenland
Walking in Norway

SLOVENIA, CROATIA AND MONTENEGRO
The Julian Alps of Slovenia
The Mountains of Montenegro
Trekking in Slovenia
Walking in Croatia

SPAIN AND PORTUGAL
Costa Blanca Walks
  1 West & 2 East
Mountain Walking in Southern
  Catalunya
The Mountains of Central Spain
Trekking through Mallorca
Via de la Plata
Walking in Madeira
Walking in Mallorca
Walking in the Algarve
Walking in the Canary Islands
  2 East
Walking in the Cordillera
  Cantabrica
Walking in the Sierra Nevada
Walking on La Gomera and El
  Hierro
Walking on La Palma
Walking the GR7 in Andalucia
Walks and Climbs in the Picos
  de Europa

SWITZERLAND
Alpine Pass Route
Central Switzerland
The Bernese Alps
Tour of the Jungfrau Region
Walking in the Valais
Walking in Ticino
Walks in the Engadine

TECHNIQUES
Geocaching
Indoor Climbing
Lightweight Camping
Map and Compass
Mountain Weather
Moveable Feasts
Rock Climbing
Sport Climbing
The Book of the Bivvy
The Hillwalker's Guide to
  Mountaineering
The Hillwalker's Manual

MINI GUIDES
Avalanche!
Navigating with a GPS
Navigation
Pocket First Aid and Wilderness
  Medicine
Snow

For full and up-to-date
information on our ever-
expanding list of guides,
visit our website:
www.cicerone.co.uk.

Cicerone's mission is to inform and inspire by providing the best guides to exploring the world

Since its foundation 40 years ago, Cicerone has specialised in publishing guidebooks and has built a reputation for quality and reliability. It now publishes nearly 300 guides to the major destinations for outdoor enthusiasts, including Europe, UK and the rest of the world.

Written by leading and committed specialists, Cicerone guides are recognised as the most authoritative. They are full of information, maps and illustrations so that the user can plan and complete a successful and safe trip or expedition – be it a long face climb, a walk over Lakeland fells, an alpine cycling tour, a Himalayan trek or a ramble in the countryside.

With a thorough introduction to assist planning, clear diagrams, maps and colour photographs to illustrate the terrain and route, and accurate and detailed text, Cicerone guides are designed for ease of use and access to the information.

If the facts on the ground change, or there is any aspect of a guide that you think we can improve, we are always delighted to hear from you.

Cicerone Press
2 Police Square Milnthorpe Cumbria LA7 7PY
Tel: 015395 62069 Fax: 015395 63417
info@cicerone.co.uk www.cicerone.co.uk